TROTSKY

The Permanent Revolutionary

MICHAEL LYNCH

Hodder & Stoughton

A MEMBER OF THE HODDER HEADLINE GROUP

ACKNOWLEDGEMENTS

The publishers would like to thank the following for their permission to reproduce illustrations in this volume:

Camera Press: cover.
David King Collection: p14; p25; p29; p45; p57; p59; p65; p80; p84; p85; p86; p108.

Every effort has been made to trace and acknowledge ownership of copyright. The publishers will be glad to make suitable arrangements with any copyright holder whom it has not been possible to contact.

British Library Cataloguing in Publication Data
Lynch, Michael
   Trotsky: Permanent Revolutionary. –
   (Personalities & Powers Series)
   I. Title II. Series
   947.084092

   ISBN 0-340-60283-x

First published 1995
Impression number   10   9   8   7   6   5   4   3   2   1
Year   1998   1997   1996   1995

Typeset by Litho Link Ltd, Welshpool, Powys, Wales.
Printed in Great Britain for Hodder and Stoughton Educational, a division of Hodder Headline Plc, 338 Euston Road, London NW1 3BH by St Edmundsbury Press, Bury St Edmunds, Suffolk.

CONTENTS

INTRODUCTION

The weather in Mexico City on 20 August 1940 was hot and dry. Yet Ramon Mercader was wearing a raincoat as he entered No.19 Avenida Viena, the heavily-guarded home of Leon Davidovich Bronstein, a 61-year-old Russian émigré. Mercader, alias Jacques Mornard, alias Frank Jacson, walked into Bronstein's study and asked him to look over an article he had brought. As Bronstein leaned forward to study it, Mercader reached into his raincoat pocket, drew out an ice-pick, and smashed it ten centimetres into the old man's head. Bronstein staggered to his feet, tugged the ice-pick from his head, and struggled with his assailant. Guards rushed in and beat Mercader to the floor. A weeping Natalya Bronstein, tried to staunch the blood pouring from the hole in her husband's skull. But the old man had sustained a mortal wound. A day later he was dead.

The murdered émigré is better known to history as Trotsky, the organiser of the Russian Revolution of 1917. He had been assassinated on the orders of Joseph Vissarionovich Dzhugashvili, better known to history as Stalin, the ruler of the USSR between 1927 and 1953. Trotsky's death provides a dramatic climax to a story that goes back to the beginning of the twentieth century.

RUSSIA AT THE BEGINNING OF THE TWENTIETH CENTURY

The Russia in which Trotsky grew up was a socially-divided and economically-backward nation. The imperial census of 1897 revealed that 82 per cent of the rapidly-growing population of 120 million were peasants. The ruling class of royals, nobles, court officials, higher clergy, and senior army officers accounted for 12 per cent. The industrial working class formed barely 4 per cent, while the commercial middle class amounted to a mere 2 per cent. These statistics, revealing the heavy preponderance of peasants in the population, help to explain why Russia had not shared in the industrial growth that was such a marked feature of western Europe in the nineteenth century.

Not only had Russia failed to develop an industrial economy; its agricultural system remained wedded to archaic, inefficient, forms of food production. Despite being legally emancipated from serfdom in 1861, the mass of the peasantry remained deeply conservative and opposed to innovation. Geography did not help. Much of the Russian empire lay within northern latitudes which limited the amount of cultivatable soil. This factor, together with rapid growth in population and the tradition of equal sub-division of land among successive generations of families, created a land hunger, which either reduced the peasants to penury or drove them in desperation into the ill-provisioned towns. Their plight was made worse by the underlying social disharmony in Russia. Among the governing classes there was an abiding contempt for the peasants and workers whose huge numbers and brutish ways made them socially dangerous. The ruling elite believed that the only way to treat these 'dark masses' was to keep them down.

Tsarist Russia was a vast empire, covering millions of square miles and stretching across half of Europe and the breadth of Asia. It contained a variety of races, languages and cultures. Standing on the periphery of eastern Europe, Russia for centuries had remained outside the mainstream of European affairs. It is true that exceptional tsars, such as Peter the Great in the eighteenth century, had modernised certain features of Russian life, but the changes were superficial. Overwhelmingly reactionary in outlook, successive tsarist governments had tried to shut out western ideas. Russian rulers had been particularly anxious to prevent the incursion of such concepts as democracy and representative government. Imperial Russia was an absolute monarchy; the tsar was the embodiment of total state authority. In Russia in 1900 it was still a crime to oppose him or his government, parliament did not exist, political parties were illegal, and newspapers and books were state controlled. Government was administered by officials drawn from a privileged social elite, who operated a bureaucracy that was both intrusive and inefficient.

The Russian Orthodox Church, a long-established power in the land and a major opponent of change, used its considerable influence over the people to enjoin them to look upon the tsar as their divinely-appointed ruler. Public order was maintained by the use of the Russian army which was more often engaged in suppressing risings within the empire than in fighting foreign wars. The control of political opposition or protest was entrusted to the *Okhrana*, the tsarist secret police; raids, arrests, and harassment were a constant feature of Russian life.

The only recourse for critics of the regime was to go underground. Such political life as there was in Russia was necessarily secretive and conspiratorial. This stifling of genuine debate had significant repercussions. Politics became a compound of oppression and violent resistance. There was no middle way; moderation and compromise were alien to the Russian tradition. Even when reforms were attempted by the more enlightened tsars, they were regarded with suspicion by the lower orders and distaste by the privileged, and were invariably followed by a period of reaction. This was typified by the example of Alexander II (1855-81). Early in his reign he tried to win over the *intelligentsia* (a general term for the educated and progressive elements in Russian society) by a series of gestures that included the relaxing of government controls on the press and on the universities. The response of the *intelligentsia* was not to show gratitude for the concessions but to demand further changes. Fearing that he had gone too far, Alexander abandoned reform and reimposed coercion. In 1881 he was blown to pieces by a terrorist bomb. It seemed that sullen obedience or violent resistance were the only possible responses to government oppression.

Despite the chronic weaknesses and the resistance to change that characterised tsarist Russia at the end of the nineteenth century, change was occurring nonetheless. A great deal was happening on the industrial front. The 1890s experienced what became known as 'the great spurt'. The production of oil, coal and iron expanded rapidly. So, too, did the railway system; by 1900 there were 53,234 miles of railway line, compared with 21,228 twenty years earlier. Considerable foreign funds were invested in Russia, and her balance of trade went significantly into credit. This was in part the result of private enterprise, but government initiatives were also important. Sergei Witte, the Minister of Finance (1893-1903) made prodigious efforts to attract foreign capital into

Russia, as the first step towards a major industrial expansion.

His endeavours were only partially successful. One reason for this was that the royal government which he was endeavouring to serve, declined to give him their full backing. The obstructions Witte faced in trying to modernise Russia illustrate a basic divide that had long confused Russia's attitude towards itself and the outside world. There were those who argued that Russia had a future as a great power only if it modernised itself on the model of the successful nations of western Europe. These 'westerners' were vehemently opposed by the 'slavo-philes', those who asserted that Russia's unique and historically-separate character had to be preserved by avoiding the taint of western ways and values. The irreconcilability of these two viewpoints had effectively prevented progressive moves being successful in Russia. It is not difficult to understand the frustration felt by those who wanted Russia to embrace change.

Such in outline was the situation in Russia as Trotsky came to maturity. What made the times so highly-charged, and gave hope to revolutionaries, was that although Russia was an absolutist tsarist autocracy in theory, it was not a very efficient one in practice. The outlawing of parties had not prevented their existence and the attempt to keep out subversive political notions had served only to increase their circulation. By the end of the nineteenth century, a range of reformist and revolutionary parties had come into being. The incompetence of the authorities was strikingly evidenced by the way they treated their political dissidents. Tsarist prisons could be very grim places but they could also be breeding grounds for the spread of the very revolutionary ideas which the incarcerations were supposed to combat. The areas in Siberia where political prisoners were exiled were often referred to as the 'universities of revolution', for it was such exile that provided the perfect circumstances for the dissemination of radical ideas among the disaffected.

By 1903, three major revolutionary movements had developed, each dedicated to the overthrow of the tsarist system.

Populism

Dating from the 1870s, the populist movement looked upon the peasants as the instruments for transforming Russia. Drawing its leaders from the enlightened middle and upper classes, the movement took as its major task the political education of the peasants, a policy known as 'going to the people'. However, despite the efforts of the intellectuals who went to live in the countryside, the conservative peasantry remained largely resistant to the revolutionary message. In frustration, a number of populists adopted terrorism as their basic strategy. Consisting originally of only some 30 members, this group, 'the People's Will', succeeded, over a period of 25 years, in assassinating over 2000 nobles and government officers; Tsar Alexander II was its most notable victim in 1881. The historical importance of populism was its role in creating a revolutionary atmosphere in imperial Russia. Both Lenin and Trotsky began their political careers as populists.

The Social Revolutionary Party (SRs)

This was largest of the parties and had grown directly out of Populism. Although the SRs were essentially a peasant-based movement, they attempted during the 1890s, the decade of rapid industrial growth and increasing political tension, to attract the factory workers in the urban areas. Victor Chernov was the leading spokesman among the SRs and as a member of the *intelligentsia* it was he who endeavoured to turn the loose ideas of Populism into a positive political programme. However, the very attempt to widen their revolutionary base created divisions and weaknesses among the SRs. Trotsky observed:

> [They were] formed at the beginning of the century from a fusion of several tendencies of the Narodniks [Populists]. Representing the wavering interests of the small peasant proprietor, the party soon split into a group of Left Social Revolutionaries, anarchist in their leanings, and the Right Social Revolutionaries.

While the anarchists continued the terror tactics of 'the People's Will', the more moderate SRs were prepared to work with the other parties for improved conditions for the workers and peasants. Despite the split in their ranks to which Trotsky referred, the truth was that the SRs remained the largest and most popular of the revolutionary parties until the Revolution of 1917.

The All-Russian Social Democratic Workers Party (SDs)

Though smaller in membership than the SRs, the SDs were the most dedicated and committed of the revolutionary groups in Russia. The party was formed in 1898 on Marxist principles. Its founding father was George Plekhanov, who 20 years earlier had set up the first Marxist organisation in Russia, 'the Group for the Emancipation of Labour'. It was through Plekhanov's translations that young revolutionaries like Lenin and Trotsky came to know the major Marxist texts. It is not difficult to appreciate why Marxism appealed to Russian revolutionaries. Central to Marx's scientific analysis of human society was the assertion that history was a matter of conflict and that all movement forward took the form of violent revolutionary struggle by the exploited class against the fiercely-resistant exploiting class. The most stimulating aspect for revolutionaries was Marx's teaching that this series of class struggles (the dialectic) had entered its final stage in the current industrial era with the conflict between the owners of capital (the bourgeoisie) and the industrial workers (the proletariat). What gave this concept special relevance and application at the turn of the century was Russia's rapid industrial expansion in the 1890s. This 'great spurt' looked set to establish in Russia the industrial conditions which would make possible a successful proletarian revolution. A growing and disaffected labour force would now provide a focus and a means of achieving a successful challenge to the bourgeoisie.

Lenin was in exile in Siberia at the time of the founding of the SD Party in 1898. When he returned to western Russia two years later he was intent on transforming the SDs into a genuinely Marxist revolutionary party. His determination to do so was to have far-reaching consequences for the whole of the Russian revolutionary movement, not least for Trotsky.

In addition to the revolutionary parties, there were also political groups who wanted change in Russia, but who believed that modernisation could be gained by the reform rather than the destruction of the existing social and political structure. Their attitude was broadly referred to as liberalism.

The Liberals

These groups, whose leaders invariably came from the *intelligentsia*, represented the small but ambitious professional classes who calculated that unless Russia were modernised they would be denied real economic and social advance. A significant number of the spokesmen of the national minorities also supported liberalism since they saw it as the best means of asserting their independence of imperial Russia. It was during the 1905 Revolution that two liberal political parties came into being, the Octobrists and the Kadets. The former took their name from the October Manifesto (see page 22), which was regarded as a significant achievement in Russian politics. The Kadets (Constitutional Democrats) were formed in May 1905 under the leadership of Paul Milyukov and they were to prove the most enduring and significant of the liberal parties. Their essential programme was to work for the inauguration of a constitutional monarchy in which the tsar's authority would be limited by an elected parliament drawn from all the constituent parts of the Russian empire. The creation of such a representative body, empowered to settle Russia's outstanding social, political and economic problems, became the major objective of all Russian liberals.

Trotsky often dismissed the liberal parties as having been left behind by the march of history, but he was not above co-operating with them when it seemed expedient.

AN OUTLINE OF TROTSKY'S CAREER

Born in 1879 into a Jewish landowning family in the Ukraine, Lev (Leon or Leib) Bronstein showed early signs of intellectual gifts. He was sent to special schools in Odessa and Nicolayev to develop his literary skills, learn foreign languages, and acquaint himself with both Russian tradition and the wider aspects of European culture. He became attracted to Marxist revolutionary ideas and in 1898 was exiled to Siberia for his involvement in organising workers' protests against the tsarist regime. He escaped four years later and fled abroad, adopting the revolutionary pseudonym of Trotsky, the name of one of his former gaolers. In London, he met Lenin for the first time and collaborated in the publication of a revolutionary journal, *Iskra* (the spark). As the SD delegate from Siberia, he attended the Second Congress of the Party in 1903. It was at this Congress that the SDs split into the Bolshevik (majority) faction, led by Lenin, and the Mensheviks (minority) led by George Plekhanov and Julius Martov. The division was as much a matter of personality differences as of political principle, but by 1912 the two wings had hardened into distinct and separate Marxist parties. Trotsky's broad sympathies lay with the Mensheviks but he was concerned that the divisions should not become irreparable.

It was as a Menshevik that Trotsky became president of the short-lived St Petersburg Soviet during the 1905 Revolution, the period of concessions made by the Tsar in the face of demands for reform, following Russia's humiliation in the war against Japan (1904−5). Trotsky was the only leading SD to come out of the 1905 Revolution with credit. Indeed, his role as leader of the Soviet is often described as the first of the three outstanding achievements of his political career. However, in the repression imposed by the tsarist regime after the crushing of the Revolution in 1906, Trotsky was again exiled, this time to an Arctic penal colony. Once more he escaped and was smuggled out of Russia. He would not return until 1917. In the intervening years he was constantly on the move: Britain, Finland, France, Austria, Spain, Switzerland and the USA were among the countries in which he took up residence. It was during these years of exile that he developed his own particular interpretation of Marxism, the theory of 'permanent revolution'.

Along with Lenin, Trotsky condemned the European war which broke out in 1914 as a struggle between the capitalist-imperialist nations. Nevertheless, the war proved greatly to the advantage of Russian revolutionaries, since it was that struggle that exposed the weaknesses of the tsarist system and made the 1917 Revolution possible. 1917 marked the second high point in Trotsky's career. The February Revolution of that year, which saw the end of tsardom and its replacement by the dual authority of the Provisional Government and the Petrograd Soviet, was the occasion for a rush of émigré revolutionaries back to Russia. Trotsky experienced delays, but when he eventually made his return he immediately joined the Bolshevik Party. In July he was arrested for his part in a premature attempt by the Bolsheviks to overthrow the Provisional Government, but was released soon after. As 1917 wore on, the Petrograd Soviet became increasingly dominated by the Bolsheviks. Trotsky was elected its chairman, a position which left him ideally placed to plot the next Bolshevik assault on the Provisional Government. This duly and successfully came in October 1917. If Lenin was undeniably the inspiration behind the October Revolution, Trotsky was indisputably the executive figure who organised the actual rising.

In the Bolshevik government that took power, Trotsky became Commissar for Foreign Affairs. He was the chief negotiator in the Russo-German negotiations that culminated with the Treaty of Brest-Litovsk

(1918), the agreement that took Russia out of the war. Soon after, came the event that occasioned the third great achievement in Trotsky's career. This was the Civil War of 1918-20, a bitter struggle between the Reds (Bolsheviks) and the Whites (a loose amalgam of all those opposed to the October Revolution) to determine whether the Bolsheviks could consolidate their hold over the new Soviet Russia. The Bolshevik success in this owed much to the performance of the Red Army under Trotsky, as Commissar for War. Although a civilian, he used his organisational and inspirational skills to turn a motley collection of troops into a highly-efficient fighting force which eventually routed the Whites.

The early 1920s were not merely a time of military trial for the Bolsheviks. The new regime also underwent enormous strains economically. Trotsky was among those leading Bolsheviks who favoured a hard line; he fully supported the policy of war communism with its repressive measures and tight political control. He was instrumental in destroying the Russian trade unions as an independent force, and in 1921 it was he who ordered the brutal suppression of the Kronstadt workers who had protested against the Bolshevik government's misuse of its power. When Lenin, faced by widespread famine, subsequently introduced the New Economic Policy (NEP), which allowed the peasants to engage in trade for profit, Trotsky publicly acquiesced, but there is doubt as to how genuinely he accepted this concession to capitalism.

Lenin's terminal illness between 1922 and 1924 meant that during the last two years of his life a jockeying for power had already begun. Yet at his death, there was still no clear successor to the leadership. In terms of sheer talent, Trotsky ought to have been a front-runner. But in some respects his very abilities were his limitations. He had never been fully accepted by his fellow Bolsheviks, who distrusted his intellectual brilliance and viewed his conversion to Bolshevism in 1917 as expedient rather than genuine. Though he had gained a following in the army and among international revolutionaries, he was distrusted by the Communist Party (CPSU) within the USSR. It became apparent in the power struggle that ensued between 1924 and 1927 that Trotsky had no power base within the CPSU. This enabled Stalin, very much the organisation man, who held a number of key positions in both government and party, to isolate Trotsky. At crucial decisions in the Politburo, the inner cabinet of the Party, Stalin was able to deliver the votes. By 1927, Trotsky had effectively lost the power struggle. His ideas on economics and his concept of permanent revolution were condemned as anti-Soviet. In 1928 he was forced into internal exile at Alma Ata. A year later he was permanently exiled from the USSR itself.

Trotsky spent his last 11 years in a variety of countries, before finally settling in Mexico. All the while he continued to write voluminously, depicting Stalin as a betrayer of the revolution of 1917, and endeavouring to develop an international following opposed to the Soviet regime. In Stalin's judgement, Trotsky in exile had a certain value to the Soviet authorities since he could be used as an all purpose hate-figure, association with whom was proof of guilt. Finally, however, Stalin came to the conclusion that as long as Trotsky remained alive he would be an affront and a danger. In 1940 he ordered the assassination that Mercader carried out.

This book is not intended as a biography of Trotsky. Its aim is to assess his role in the Russian Revolution and to offer an analysis of his particular brand of Marxism, the theory of 'permanent revolution'. In recent years, following the disintegration of the USSR and the collapse of the Communist regimes in the Eastern Bloc, the whole period of the Russian Revolution has come in for reappraisal. One fascinating aspect of this has been the quickening of interest in Leon Trotsky and his particular interpretation of Marxist theory. If he, rather than Stalin, had won the power struggle in the post-Lenin years would the USSR have been saved from the horrors and failures it subsequently experienced? Would revolution have developed a human face? Would the Soviet Union have developed into the first truly successful Marxist state? Indeed, would he, as Trotskyists claim, have led the way to world revolution? The frequency with which such questions are asked testifies to Trotsky's abiding significance.

TROTSKY, MENSHEVISM AND BOLSHEVISM

TROTSKY'S BACKGROUND

Trotsky's family were Jewish, but not typically so. Most Jews in imperial Russia lived either in towns or as poor agricultural labourers. The Bronsteins, however, owned land. In the period following Trotsky's exile from Russia in 1929 it became the norm to dismiss his father as having been a 'kulak' (a rich exploiting peasant landowner). The truth is that David Bronstein did employ workers, but the Bronsteins were hardly a wealthy family. They had clawed their way to relative comfort, but as Jews their prospects of obtaining real wealth in tsarist Russia were very small. Jews were legally restricted to living in particular areas (known as the Pale of Settlement) and they were debarred from a whole range of public positions and offices. This discrimination was part of a long-established anti-Semitic tradition which frequently expressed itself in violent, state-organised, pogroms. That, indeed, was one of the explanations why so many Jews were to be found in the ranks of the revolutionaries. In 1897 a separate Jewish revolutionary organisation was formed, known as the Bund.

Significantly, Trotsky chose not to join it. This was one example of his persistence throughout his career in denying his own Jewishness. He could not, of course, change his racial origins, but he declined to belong to Judaism as a creed or a culture. In later life he wrote, 'My Jewishness never played a leading part – nor even a recognised one – in the list of my grievances'. As a declared atheist and materialist he found the traditional Judaic emphasis on religion and spirituality to be distasteful.

Moreover, while he may not have been able to change his race he could disown it. During his period as a Commissar in the Bolshevik government, a delegation of Jews came to beg him to use his influence to lessen the widespread persecution of their people; he dismissed them with the words. 'I am not a Jew, but an internationalist'. Trotsky was in good revolutionary company. It had been Karl Marx, himself a Jew, who had condemned the Jews as a grasping, corrupting, element within society. Yet, in spite of their disclaimers, both Marx and Trotsky were deeply influenced by their racial origins. A modern Jewish scholar, Nora Levin, has explained why secular Jews like Trotsky were drawn into revolutionary politics in Russia:

> Bolshevism attracted marginal Jews, poised between two worlds - the Jewish and the Gentile - who created a new homeland for themselves, a community of ideologists bent on remaking the world in their own image. These Jews quite deliberately and consciously broke with the restrictive social, religious, and cultural life of the Jews in the Pale of Settlement . . . the Jewish Bolsheviks found their ideological home in revolutionary universalism.

HIS FORMATIVE YEARS

Leon Bronstein was a short-sighted youth, proud of wearing spectacles since he felt it made him look intellectual. He suffered from colic, which at times, was so intense that he was often obliged to miss school. There are strong suggestions, however, that his illnesses were imaginary or self-induced. They do seem to have afflicted him at particularly-critical points in his career.

A bright child from the first, he was a keen observer of all that went on around him. We learn from his autobiography that he had a natural sympathy for the peasants who worked on the family estate. Their lot was hard; they were chronically short of food and creature comforts. One day a group of them showed their sense of desperation by lying in front of Trotsky's father and slowly waving their bare, cracked, and bleeding feet in the air. David Bronstein was moved by the plight of these men; he brought out some wine for them and promised to help when he could. It is not suggested that this was the type of experience that turned Trotsky into a revolutionary. The truth was that he approached the question of privilege and deprivation very much as an intellectual. He was not concerned with the amelioration of suffering at an individual level. Indeed, suffering was highly valuable socially in that it intensified the sense of grievance of the downtrodden and sharpened their taste for revolution. Trotsky shared with Lenin a distaste for what they called 'economism', that is the movement which sought to raise the standards of peasants and workers by improving their living and working conditions. Revolution was an affair of class against class. Antagonisms had to be deepened by exploiting grievances, not lessened by introducing reforms. The revolutionary slogan, 'the worse it is, the better it is' encapsulates their attitude.

While living in Odessa and Nikolayev, where he had been sent to be educated, Trotsky came into contact with a range of cultural influences that helped to shape his young mind. He developed a taste for art and Italian opera and extended his appreciation of foreign literary classics. His developing artistic and intellectual tastes put him at variance with his poorly-educated parents. Although they admired their son and took pride in his achievements, it is doubtful whether they ever really understood him. By the age of 17, Trotsky had fallen out with his father. David Bronstein viewed his son's daily round of animated discussions and debates with his revolutionary friends as mere dilettantism.

Between 1896 and 1898 Trotsky spent his time writing and studying. He dropped his earlier Populism and embraced Marxism as an ideology. He corresponded with revolutionaries abroad, and helped to form the Southern Worker's Union in 1897, dedicated to agitating against employers. In 1898 the inevitable occurred. He was arrested and, after being held in a number of Ukrainian prisons, was exiled to Siberia, the common fate of opponents of the tsarist regime. Life in Siberia was not especially severe; the punishment was the exile itself. The authorities hoped that, by removing dissidents thousands of miles from Moscow or St Petersburg or Kiev, rebellion could be contained. What happened was almost the exact opposite. The Siberian settlements became breeding grounds for revolution.

By 1902, anxious not to lose touch with what he judged to be important developments among the revolutionaries in western Europe, Trotsky resolved to escape. With the blessing of his wife, Alexandra Sokolovskya, whom he had married during his first year of exile, he left her and their two children behind and made his arduous way first to St

ИСКРА

Пролетарiи всѣхъ странъ, соединяйтесь!

...Изъ искры возгорится пламя!...

Центральный Органъ Россiйской Соцiальдемократической Рабочей Партiи

№ 62. 15-го марта 1904 г. Годъ IV.

Iskra, the revolutionary journal which Trotsky helped to edit

Petersburg and then to London. In the course of his journeys he met Axelrod, a revolutionary whose reputation he already admired. It was in London in 1902, however, that he spent a number of weeks with the outstanding revolutionary of the age, Lenin. Although the two were subsequently to have their differences, mutual respect appears to have been there from the first. Lenin was instrumental in having Trotsky placed on the editorial board of *Iskra*, the SD journal, despite the protests of some of the more established members. Trotsky was also sent on a lecture tour to a number of European cities including Paris. He was markedly impressed by the high culture which he experienced. His travels were a further refinement of his educated sensibilities, but his thirst for revolution remained undimmed.

THE SD SPLIT
—

Since its inception five years earlier, conflicting ideas had developed within the SD party as to how it could best fulfil its Marxist revolutionary mission. Lenin and Julius Martov had founded *Iskra* to urge a much more aggressive approach by the SDs. Lenin's concern was that the young party might move towards 'economism', concerning itself with trade unionism and reform of conditions, to the neglect of its revolutionary purpose. It was the *Iskra* editorial board, on which Trotsky sat, that was responsible for convening the SD Congress in 1903. The main agenda was to determine the character and structure of the party. It proved to be a momentous gathering; from it emerged the two major contending Marxist parties, the Mensheviks and the Bolsheviks. It was at this Congress that Trotsky and Stalin met for the first time. In later life Trotsky denied all memory of the meeting, but Stalin claimed to remember it well.

The Congress, which met first in Brussels and then moved to Limehouse in London in order to avoid police surveillance, had its comic side. One session had to be suspended when the delegates were attacked by fleas that infested the rotten furniture in the warehouse where they had gathered. The London authorities looked on tolerantly, if quizzically, at these funny foreign gentlemen whose idea of discussion seemed to be to shout at each other at the top of their voices.

The fundamental question to be discussed was one of organisation. How could an émigré party so shape itself as to be in a position to achieve revolution when the opportunity presented itself? Of the many confused responses that emerged at the Congress, the clearest and ultimately the most dominant was Lenin's. His answer was that the Party must be a tightly-organised, dedicated, grouping of professional revolutionaries, in agreement on all essentials and prepared to obey instructions from the leaders of the Party. Lenin is renowned for having contributed to Marxism the principle of the party as the vanguard of revolution. Marx had said little about the way revolution was to be practically organised. His celebrated admonition 'Worker's Of The World Unite!' was a general appeal to a class not to an organising group.

Lenin set himself the task of translating Marxism into a practical programme. Given the nature of tsarist absolutism, revolution had to be planned in exile. That was why the issue of the party's structure was so critical, as, too, were the questions of loyalty and discipline in regard to party orders.

Lenin wrote *What Is To Be Done?* in 1902 in order to undermine those SDs, such as Plekhanov and Martov, who advocated pursuing a broad combination of all the revolutionary and progressive elements in Russia. He followed the same line at the Congress, insisting that the revolution could be prepared only by a single, close-knit, and disciplined party whose understanding of the science of the dialectic gave it the sole right to determine policy. He reasoned that the proletariat could not organise revolution by themselves; they required direction and leadership. Although he often affected to despise intellectuals, Lenin was utterly convinced that it was only from the *intelligentsia* that the necessary revolutionary leadership would come.

> The history of every country teaches us that by its own ability the working class can attain only a trade-unionist self-consciousness . . . The Socialist doctrine, on the other hand, is the outgrowth of those philosophical, historical and economic theories which had been developed by the representatives of the well to do, the intellectuals.
>
> The blind unfolding of the labour movement can lead only to the permeation of that movement with a bourgeois ideology, because the unconscious growth of the labour movement . . . signifies the mental enslavement of the workers to the bourgeoisie. Therefore our task as Social Democrats is to oppose this blind process, to divert the labour movement from the unconscious tendency of trade unionism to march under the protective wing of the bourgeoisie and to bring it under the influence of Social Democracy instead.

Although most SDs wished to avoid an open split in the party, Lenin adopted a deliberately confrontational approach, forcing the delegates to take sides on a range of what in themselves were minor procedural matters. The most divisive issue concerned the qualifications necessary for membership of the SD Party. In the heated debates Martov, who had previously been Lenin's closest colleague, became his chief adversary. He was convinced that Lenin was bent on becoming dictator of the party. Martov challenged Lenin's notion of professional exclusiveness and argued for a party open to all progressives and radicals.

The essence of Lenin's rationale was that unless the party insisted on a tightly-restricted membership the scattered revolutionaries would lack a focus for their loyalty; ideas would abound and orthodoxy would become impossible to maintain. For émigrés, a disciplined, centralised, party was a matter of necessity not of choice. There was the further vital corollary that, since the party was necessarily a structured body with authority vested in its central committee, obedience was owed ultimately by members to that central body. The authoritarian implications of this 'democratic centralism' were clear, but Lenin made no effort to deny them. His argument was that, left to themselves, the members could not run the party any more than the masses could lead a revolution; neither group would know how.

In the course of the Congress, the points of view represented by Lenin and Martov became classified respectively as Bolshevik (majority) and Menshevik (minority). The terms did not in fact accurately illustrate the support that each of the protagonists had; they were titles first employed by Lenin after winning a particular set of votes on minor resolutions. But the labels stuck, to become in time the names of two distinct parties. That they did so was due less to ideological differences among the SDs than to Lenin's characteristic determination not to tolerate opposition. In the division between Bolsheviks and Mensheviks the *Iskra* editorial board, which included Trotsky, were all members of the latter group. Lenin chose to perpetuate this divide by abandoning *Iskra* and starting his own journal *Vyperod* (Forward) with which to attack the Mensheviks. During the next two years Lenin intrigued against his former SD allies; his aim was to establish himself as the only truly Marxist leader at the head of a party wholly subordinate to his wishes. Ironically, throughout the period between 1903 and 1917 the Mensheviks were to be the larger and more popular of the two parties that Lenin's actions had forced into being.

At the time of the 1903 split, there was little doubt where Trotsky's sympathies lay. Immediately after the event he wrote a number of essays and pamphlets highly critical of Lenin, whom he likened to Robespierre, the power-hungry leader of the Jacobins in the French Revolution of 1789.

Who could suppose that this [Congress], convened by *Iskra*, would mercilessly trample over *Iskra's* editorial board . . . this man with the energy and talent peculiar to him, assumed the role of the party's disorganizer ... We suffered defeat because fate has decreed victory not for centralism but for self-centredness.

Lenin's methods lead to this: the party organisation at first substitutes itself for the party as a whole; then the Central Committee substitutes itself for the organisation; and finally a single 'dictator' substitutes himself for the Central Committee.

After 1917 Trotsky was concerned to apologise for having opposed Lenin during the pre-revolutionary years. The Bolshevik success in the October Revolution seemed to prove that Lenin had been right all along and it threw a dark shadow over those who had not fully supported him before 1917. This subsequently made those ex-Mensheviks with a dubious past seek to be more Leninist than Lenin. One of the reasons why Trotsky was never fully trusted by his Bolshevik colleagues was that they doubted the sincerity of his sudden conversion to Leninism in July 1917. They judged it as mere expediency on his part. The idea of Trotsky as an outsider dogged him throughout his career. He was aware of this and doubtless his avoidance of involvement in Jewish questions was a way of attempting to avoid further isolation.

timeline	1879	Lev Bronstein born into a Jewish landed family in the southern Ukraine
	1888-98	educated in Odessa and Nikolayev; becomes actively involved in revolutionary agitation
	1898	convicted of political offences and exiled to Siberia; he marries Alexandra Sokolovskaya there; has two daughters
	1902	escapes, adopting the revolutionary name, Trotsky, and flees to London where he joins Lenin and other leading Marxist revolutionaries; edits *Iskra*; meets Natalya Sedova
	1903	attends 2nd Congress of SDs in Brussels; sides with the Mensheviks in Bolshevik-Menshevik split

Points to consider

1) In what respects was Trotsky's Jewishness a factor in his becoming a revolutionary?
2) Why was Trotsky opposed to 'economism'?
3) For what reasons did Lenin enforce a split in the ranks of the SDs at the 1903 Congress in London?
4) How widely did Trotsky differ from Lenin on the question of party membership and structure?

TROTSKY AND THE 1905
REVOLUTION

In 1905 came the most serious challenge yet encountered by the tsarist regime in its 300 year history. January 1905 witnessed the brutal dispersal by government forces of a workers' demonstration. The incident, known as 'Bloody Sunday', began a build-up of violent protest, which took the form in the succeeding months of widespread strikes, land seizures, the open formation of opposition parties, assertions of independence by the national minorities, and mutiny in the armed forces. All this occurred against the backdrop of a humiliatingly-unsuccessful war against Japan. By the autumn, Tsar Nicholas II was obliged to placate his opponents by issuing the 'October Manifesto' in which he granted a number of concessions.

THE RUSSIAN REVOLUTION OF 1905

Although Bloody Sunday is traditionally taken as the start of the 1905 revolution, a great deal had happened before that event to create an atmosphere of confrontation. The revolution did not come out of the blue. Worker misery and peasant anxieties were contributory factors, but it was also a product of university unrest and agitation by the *zemstvos* (elected local councils). It is not surprising that the universities should have bred open opposition to the government. In the period of sharp reaction following the assassination of Alexander II in 1881, severe restrictions had been reimposed on the universities. Student resistance built up in reaction and became particularly marked by the turn of the century. Prince Trubetskoi, the rector of Moscow University, described the university protests as the beginning of 'the general crisis of the state'.

The tsarist authorities were equally disturbed by the rebellious actions of the *zemstvos*. These councils had come into being in the reforming period of the 1860s as the first formal expression of democratic activity in local government. The tsarist government had hoped that they would prove a source of stability and order in the state. But the reverse seemed to be the case. Throughout 1904 the *zemstvos* leaders held a series of banquets, modelled on the French revolutionary tradition; at these functions it became the rule to criticise the regime and press for further freedoms to be granted.

The assassination of Plehve, the Minister of the Interior, by the SRs in July 1904, was a graphic expression of the underlying mood of frustration. Peter Struve, a former revolutionary, described the violence as 'the logical development of a moribund autocracy'.

> Russian autocracy, in the person of its last two tsars and their ministers, has stubbornly cut off the country from all avenues of legal and gradual political development . . . The terrible thing for the government . . . is the public atmosphere of resentment and indignation which these bearers of authority create and which breeds in the ranks of Russian society one avenger after another.

Given this growing tension, Bloody Sunday, which might otherwise have been just another entry in the catalogue of tsarist repression, became the pretext for a widespread challenge to the government. In addition to widespread strikes, there was a marked increase in terrorism, much of it organised by the SRs who targeted landlords and officials as their victims. Depressing news of Russian defeats at Japanese hands provided further excuse for attacks upon the government. In May, the liberals formally organised themselves into a 'Union of Unions'; this was a Kadet initiative which aimed to draw together all those seeking reform in Russia. The mutiny of the crew of the Battleship *Prince Potemkin* in June was particularly disturbing, since for any government the loyalty of its armed forces is its last line of defence.

What made 1905 worthy of the description 'revolution' was that the three key social groups in Russia, the peasantry, the liberal middle class, and the industrial workers had come together in making their demands.

Faced with this combination, Nicholas II reluctantly issued the 'October Manifesto'. In this, in addition to granting a number of civil freedoms, he promised to set up a duma (parliament) which would possess legislative powers. A month later, the government let it be known that the mortgage repayments on land, the bane of the peasants' existence, were to be cut or abolished altogether. These were seen as highly significant concessions. The tsarist government appeared to have accepted defeat. But as subsequent events soon showed, the story was far from over.

TROTSKY'S ROLE

Trotsky was one of the few leading SDs who appeared to see the real significance of the developments which followed Bloody Sunday. It is unlikely that he believed that 1905 was the climactic revolution for which revolutionaries had been waiting. He later described it as a 'rehearsal'. Nevertheless he was anxious to seize whatever chance he could to put revolutionary theory into practice. He was in Switzerland when he heard the news of Bloody Sunday. His first reaction was one of intense excitement.

> Yes, she has come. We have awaited her. We have never doubted her. For many years she was only a deduction from doctrine; at which the non-entities of every political shade mocked . . . One day of revolution was enough, one magnificent contact between the Tsar and the people was enough for the idea of constitutional monarchy to become fantastic, doctrinaire and disgusting . . . The real monarch has destroyed the idea of the monarch . . . The revolution has come and she has put an end to our political childhood.

Within a month, in disguise and with a false passport, he was in St Petersburg. As he was unable to live openly in the city, he took up residence in Finland, just 20 miles away. From there he watched impatiently and excitedly, hoping the opportunity would arise for him to return and take an active part in the unfolding events. Although Trotsky publicly condemned the liberal reformist motions of such liberal groups as Milyukov's Kadets, he was prepared to co-operate with them in order to further the chances of revolution.

A development then occurred that was eventually to give Trotsky a major role in the revolution. Oddly enough it was initiated by the government itself. In February, a government commission, which had been set up to investigate Bloody Sunday, took the unprecedented step of inviting workers' representatives from the factories to give evidence. This was the first formal recognition of the workers as a legitimate body. The election of representatives from among the workers set the precedent for the development of the St Petersburg Workers' Soviet. This body came into being in October in the wake of the general strike of that month. From the deputies elected by the workers in the factories, an executive committee of 50 members was appointed. A stage had thus been created on which the revolutionaries could play a part in the 1905 revolution. Although the SDs and the SRs were in a minority on the committee the determination and enthusiasm they brought to their task soon made them the leading members of the Soviet. During the 50 days of the Soviet's existence, Trotsky became its outstanding figure. As Chairman, his was the voice and personality that commanded attention.

It so happened that Trotsky's direct involvement with the revolution in October coincided with the government's recovery of nerve and its determination to win back the ground it had lost. It had never been the government's genuine intention to allow an encroachment upon its authority. With the ending of the war against Japan in September 1905 and the return to Russia in the autumn of troops loyal to the regime, the tsar felt able to face down his remaining enemies. The approach adopted was very much that of divide and rule. The government had calculated that, while it would have to give way on some of the demands, if the opposition that had arisen could be bought or frightened off then the fragile link that had brought the three sections together could be broken. On Witte's advice, the tsar issued the October Manifesto in which he accepted the creation of a duma, invested with legislative powers. If the liberals could be satisfied with the offer of a duma and the peasants be pacified with the redemption of their mortgages, it would be then much easier for the government to pick off the third group, the industrial workers.

Trotsky appreciated the real situation. He pointed out to the reformers that in their enthusiasm to accept the October Manifesto they had not realised that it specifically avoided offering a constitution that weakened tsarist power. The October constitution gave the people the shadow not the substance of power.

As for the Tsar's manifesto, look, it is only a scrap of paper. Here it is before you – here it is crumpled in my fist. Today they have issued it, tomorrow they will take it away, and tear it into pieces, just as I am now tearing up this paper freedom before your eyes ... And so we have been given a constitution. We have been given freedom of assembly, but our assemblies are encircled by troops. We have been given freedom of speech, but censorship remains inviolate. We have been given freedom of study, but the universities are occupied by troops. We have been given personal immunity, but the prisons are filled to overflowing with prisoners. We have been given Witte, but we still have Trepov [the new Interior Minister]. We have been given a constitution, but the autocracy remains. Everything has been given, and nothing has been given.

Events soon bore out Trotsky's analysis. In the autumn of 1905, tsarist troops and police were used to crush resistance in the towns and factories. Anti-Jewish pogroms were actively promoted by the government as a way of diverting peasant and worker anger onto an easy target. Having barely tolerated the existence of the St Petersburg Soviet for six weeks, the government in late November ordered its closure and the arrest of its leaders. Trotsky led his colleagues in stubborn defiance. The doomed Soviet tried to organise another general strike but, despite being supported by the Union of Unions, the effort failed. By the first week of December the Soviet had been dispersed and Trotsky and his fellow deputies imprisoned to await trial. The end of the Soviet in the Russian capital was the prelude to the crushing of all the other soviets which had been formed on the St Petersburg model. It was an interesting commentary on the impotence of the Bolsheviks in 1905 that Lenin should have returned to Russia only in December, just in time to be an eye-witness at the burning of the building from which the Moscow Soviet had been driven. It is notable that such support for the revolution as came from the radical parties was provided by the Mensheviks, not the Bolsheviks. Initially the Bolsheviks had boycotted the Soviet on the grounds that they opposed the formation 'of organs of proletarian self-rule before power had been achieved'.

Given that the St Petersburg Soviet came into being only after the regime had recovered its strength of purpose, it is not surprising that it

The convicted leaders of the 1905 St Petersburg Soviet. Trotsky is marked with a cross.

should have apparently achieved so little. None of its resolutions or decisions had any meaning after it had been forcibly dissolved. Nevertheless, as Trotsky eagerly stressed, the very establishment of the Soviet had created a legacy for future revolution.

> The soviet of workers' deputies emerged in fulfilment of an objective need – generated by the course of events – for an organisation that would represent authority without containing tradition; for an organisation ready to encompass the scattered masses numbering hundreds of thousands without imposing on them many organisational restraints; for an organisation that would unite revolutionary currents within the proletariat, that could take the initiative and automatically control itself; and, most importantly, for an organisation that could be created within 24 hours.

Trotsky's imprisonment, pending his trial, was not uncongenial to him. He spent the time writing on revolution. He was able to refer to the severe reprisals undertaken by the government in 1906 against students and workers as clear proof that in no respect had the repressive character of the tsarist regime been altered by the supposed 1905 Revolution. Strength was given to Trotsky's argument by the tsar's declaration of the Fundamental Laws, which were promulgated to coincide with the opening of the first duma in April 1906 and were meant to keep the new parliament very much in its place:

> Nicholas II reasserted his unchallengeable power as head of state.
>
> The Fundamental Laws may be subject to revision in the State Council and the State Duma only on His initiative. The Sovereign Emperor ratifies the laws. No law can come into force without his approval.

Tsardom showed its true colours from 1906 onwards. The Dumas between 1906 and 1914 may have given an impression of constitutionalism, but in practice they were never a serious brake upon royal authority.

After being held in various prisons, Trotsky was eventually brought to trial in September 1906. The magistrates would have liked the proceedings to have been swift and quiet, but Trotsky embraced the opportunity to present himself and his fellow members of the Soviet as martyrs in the proletarian cause. From the dock, he delivered a series of skilfully-crafted addresses in which he told his judges that history was on his side and that the actions for which he was being tried were merely the first step towards an unstoppable revolution. Trotsky's trial speeches offer an insight into his thoughts on the nature of the revolutionary process. It is unlikely that he truly believed that full-scale revolution was imminent, but he was not going to waste the chance that the trial gave him to advance his particular interpretation of revolution.

> An insurrection of the masses, gentlemen of the bench, is not made: it accomplishes itself. It is the result of social relations, not of a scheme drawn up on paper. It cannot be created; it can only be foreseen . . . For reasons that are as little dependent on us as on tsardom, an open conflict has become inevitable . . .
>
> This, and only this, ensures the victory of a popular rising. And this is why, in our opinion, a popular rising has been 'prepared', not when the people have been armed with rifles and guns – for in that case it would never be prepared – but when it is armed with readiness to die in open street battle.

The prosecution invites us to admit that the Soviet armed the workers for the struggle against the existing 'form of government'. If I am categorically asked whether this was so, I shall answer: Yes! Yes, I am willing to accept this accusation, but on one condition only ... What we have is not a national government but an automaton for mass murder. I can find no other name for the government machine which is tearing into parts the living body of our country.

The verdict of guilty, delivered against him in November, was a foregone conclusion. He was sentenced to exile for life in Siberia. He let it be known that despite his sentence he did not intend to remain exiled for long. He was true to his word. In February 1907, while being escorted to Siberia, he made his escape. The manner of his flight is illuminating; it involved his relying on assistance from a number of peasants. He had to hide for days, buried beneath a pile of rags, while he was conveyed on a sledge. The bibulous driver frequently stopped to relieve himself. Trotsky was angered by this and recalled in his autobiography how he continually prodded and kicked the driver to prevent him from falling asleep or turning over the sledge. In his description, Trotsky could not contain his contempt for this worthless peasant, a striking illustration of the difference in Trotsky's veneration of 'the people' as a class and his treatment of them as individuals.

In his later books, *1905*, and *The History of the Russian Revolution*, Trotsky clearly defined the character of the 1905 Revolution and why it had failed. He wrote that although the tsarist regime, weakened by its humiliation in the Russo-Japanese war, had reeled for a time in the face of the opposition forces at home, it had never truly been in danger of collapse. This was because those forces were inexperienced and only superficially united. Moreover the liberals, frightened by the revolutionary movement they had unwittingly stimulated, quickly backed off and betrayed the workers. The result was that, although the experience of 1905 did leave a legend on which the 1917 revolutionaries could build, the tsarist system emerged from the 1905 Revolution stronger not weaker:

The liberals backed away from the revolution exactly at the moment when it became clear that to shake tsardom would not be enough, it must be overthrown. This sharp break of the bourgeoisie with the people, in which the bourgeoisie carried with it considerable circles of the democratic intelligentsia, made it easier for the monarchy to differentiate within the army, separating out the loyal units, and to make a bloody settlement with the workers and peasants. Although with a few broken ribs, tsarism came out of the experience of 1905 alive and strong enough.

Of Trotsky's own part in the events of 1905, perhaps the best description comes not from him but from Lunacharsky, the Bolshevik who was to become Commissar for Culture in Lenin's government in 1917.

Trotsky's popularity among the Petersburg proletariat up to the time of his arrest was very great, and it increased as a result of his extraordinarily picturesque and heroic conduct in court. I ought to say that Trotsky of all the social democratic leaders of 1905 and 1906, undoubtedly showed himself, inspite of his youth, the most thoroughly prepared; least of all, he wore the imprint of a certain emigrant narrowness, which ... impeded Lenin at that time; he more than any other realised what a broad struggle for sovereignty really is. And he came out of the revolution with the greatest gain in popularity. Neither Lenin nor Martov made any essential gain . . . Trotsky from the first stood in the front rank.

timeline	1905	Trotsky returns to St Petersburg following Bloody Sunday; active in revolutionary agitation; becomes chairman of the St Petersburg Soviet; arrested and imprisoned
	1906	convicted and exiled for life to Siberia
	1907	escapes and flees abroad

Points to consider

1) How far do the events of 1905 in Russia merit the term 'revolution'?
2) On what grounds did Trotsky condemn the 'October Manifesto'?
3) Why did the Bolsheviks play such a limited role in the 1905 Revolution?
4) What can be learned from the attitude and testimony of Trotsky at his trial concerning his understanding of the revolutionary process?

4

TROTSKY AND PERMANENT REVOLUTION

In the aftermath of the events of 1905–6, Trotsky, in consultation with the German revolutionary, Alexander Helphand (also known as 'Parvus'), began to develop a theory of Marxist revolution appropriate to Russia's particular conditions. It was a theme on which he continued to write throughout his career and one which is particularly associated with his name. It is usually referred to as the theory of 'permanent revolution', though he originally termed it 'uninterrupted revolution'. To understand it we need to examine certain key Marxist ideas.

Trotsky as a young revolutionary, with Alexander Helphand ('Parvus')

REVOLUTIONARY CLASS STRUGGLE

Marx had spoken of revolution occurring in the form of class conflict. In the course of the dialectical struggle, as the proletarian forces became stronger they would engage in violent combat with the established bourgeoisie, the current holders of power. Essential to this concept was the notion of class as the determinant of change. This raised the difficulty of how individual nations related to this pattern. Marxism taught that nations were insignificant in revolutionary terms; it was classes existing across national boundaries that mattered. Nations would disappear with the onset of revolution. Marx was, however, sufficent of a realist to appreciate that not all nations were at the same stage of economic growth and that, therefore, the degree of class development and class consciousness varied from country to country.

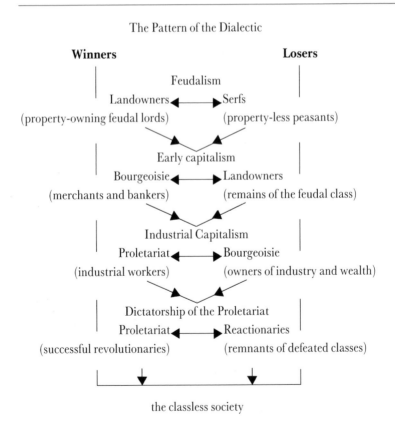

The Pattern of the Dialectic

Winners		Losers
	Feudalism	
Landowners	⟷	Serfs
(property-owning feudal lords)		(property-less peasants)
	Early capitalism	
Bourgeoisie	⟷	Landowners
(merchants and bankers)		(remains of the feudal class)
	Industrial Capitalism	
Proletariat	⟷	Bourgeoisie
(industrial workers)		(owners of industry and wealth)
	Dictatorship of the Proletariat	
Proletariat	⟷	Reactionaries
(successful revolutionaries)		(remnants of defeated classes)

the classless society

Marx had shown perception when examining the situation of Russia. He was aware that Russia's economic backwardness made her different from the advanced western European nations. In his judgement, Russia could not follow the ordinary pattern of capitalist development. Instead, it would have to go through a much slower historical development, growing from its present feudal-peasant stage to early capitalism, before reaching the stage of advanced capitalism. Marx and Engels both admired the extremist movements in Russia, in particular 'the People's Will', whose terrorism they regarded as a particularly appropriate strategy in a tsarist autocracy.

Lenin, however, considered it possible that in Russia the bourgeois and capitalist phase could be fused or 'telescoped'; this would allow the country to move directly to the proletarian revolution, which would involve the peasantry as a revolutionary force, acting in conjunction with the workers. Plekhanov, 'the father of Russian Marxism' was unhappy with this gloss on standard Marxism. He rejected the concept of revolution based on the peasants and declined to support 'the People's Will', not out of moral scruple but because indiscriminate murder would not advance the workers' revolution. Plekhanov believed that Russia could not escape the bourgeois-capitalist phase of the dialectic; without such a phase there would be no industrial proletariat, and hence no genuine development of socialism.

THE REVOLUTIONARY MENTALITY
———

Plekhanov's irritation with re-interpretations of Marxism is an interesting example of the importance of theory to revolutionaries. Their debate often seems pedantic squabbling over definitions and terms, but behind it lay a much deeper concern. What they were discussing was nothing less than the way history and human society works. They held that one could not play fancy free with the laws that govern the dialectic. To do so would be to abandon the science that made the whole of revolutionary theory valid. The bitter arguments that run throughout the history of the revolutionary parties is best likened to the theological disputes among the followers of a dogmatic religion. Concepts of truth and falsehood, orthodoxy and heresy, proliferate. It would not be an exaggeration to speak of revolutionaries seeking and defending 'the true faith'. In terms of dedication, zeal and intolerance, the revolutionary instinct was akin to the religious impulse. Lunarcharsky went so far as to describe revolutionary socialism as a mystical experience, a form of 'religious labour'.

However, underpinning such beliefs, no matter how visionary they might be, was the conviction that they were scientifically valid. We must remember that Marxism was born in an age which put an immense value on scientific discovery. The nineteenth century was greatly excited by the thought that science could unlock the door to universal knowledge. Living in the late twentieth century, with our awareness of the failure of communism as an economic and political system, we perhaps too readily forget the intoxification experienced by Marxists when they contemplated the certainties of the dialectic. Applied Marxism has become synonymous with political oppression and economic misery, but its original appeal was as a theory of liberation. Once mankind had gained control over its own situation, exploitation would end and human suffering would be extinguished. The notion that history was pre-ordained and that they were the instruments of its ordination gave revolutionaries an utter confidence that their cause would ultimately triumph. The power of this belief is the most notable characteristic of such men as Trotsky and Lenin. However low their political fortunes might appear to have sunk in the pre-1917 years they never doubted that the dynamic of history was on their side. For Trotsky, it was essentially an intellectual conviction that was proof against the accident of events. Richard Pipe's modern study contains this striking anaysis of the revolutionary mentality:

> Theories and programs, on which Russian intellectuals spent their waking hours, were indeed evaluated in relation not to life but to other theories and programs: the criterion of their validity was consistency and conformity. Live reality was treated as a perversion or caricature of 'genuine' reality, believed to lurk invisible behind appearances. This attitude would enable the intelligentsia to accept as true, propositions at total variance with demonstrable facts as well as common sense – for example, that . . . freedom meant bowing to necessity.

TROTSKY'S INTERPRETATION OF REVOLUTION

In later life Trotsky described the beliefs that had motivated him as a young revolutionary:

> The dull empiricism, the unashamed, cringing, worship of the fact were odious to me. Beyond the facts I looked for laws . . . In every sphere I felt that I could move and act only when I held in my hand the thread of the general. The social revolutionary radicalism which has become the permanent pivot for my whole inner life grew out of this intellectual enmity toward the striving for petty ends, toward out-and-out pragmatism, toward all that is ideologically without form and theoretically ungeneralised.

Paradoxically, this dominance of rational thought over feeling intensified Trotsky's passionate commitment to active politics. Convinced by his own arguments that the ends he sought had absolute value, he was untroubled by the unscrupulous means that might be necessary to achieve them, for the goal he sought was nothing less than the perfecting of the human being.

> Communist life will not be formed blindly, like coral reefs, but it will be built consciously, it will be tested by thought, it will be directed and corrected. Having ceased to be spontaneous, life will cease to be stagnant.
>
> Man will, at last, begin to harmonize himself in earnest . . . He will want to master first the semi-conscious and then also the unconscious processes of his own organism . . . The human species, the sluggish *Homo sapiens*, will once again enter the state of radical reconstruction . . . Man will make it his goal to master his own emotions, to elevate his instincts to the heights of consciousness, to make them transparent . . . to create a higher sociobiological type, a superman, if you will . . . Man will become incomparably stronger, wiser, subtler . . . The average human type will rise to the heights of an Aristotle, Goethe, Marx. And beyond this ridge, other peaks will emerge.

Trotsky took his experience of the 1905 Revolution as the starting point for his analysis of the place of Russia in the dialectic. He was well aware that 1905 had been initiated and directed by liberal and moderate reformers. Until October the revolutionaries played no part; it had been very much a case of the revolutionaries' clinging to the coat tails of the liberals. But the liberals had then betrayed the revolution by allowing themselves to be bought off by the tsarist government which had then turned on the exposed workers and defeated them. For Trotsky this raised the basic question: was the Russian proletariat really advanced enough to fulfil its role in the Marxist projection of revolution? This question went to the heart of Marxist theory.

Trotsky's reading of the theory and of the events of 1905–6 led him to the following conclusions. Given the existence of a large number of classes in society at any one time, the simple division between the dominant and exploited class becomes blurred. The principle of uneven development means that in different countries at different times classes develop at different speeds. The consequence is that when real revolution occurs it cannot be a single event; it must in the nature of things be on-going, otherwise the forces of reaction would regather and suppress it, as had happened in Russia in 1906. Trotsky was aware how important was the differing pace of proletarian growth in the various European countries. He was consistent in emphasising that this social and economic fact constrained and determined the ways in which revolution could be pursued. Tactics would vary according to the situation. Nonetheless, revolution in its broadest sense must be continuous. Revolution was not an event but a process. Once started it could not be stopped. It was in this sense that it was 'permanent'. Complementary to this concept, was his notion of revolution as an international phenomenon. His Russian experience taught him that proletarian revolution could not survive for long in one country only, since the powers of reaction would be too strong for it.

> The fundamental and most stable feature of Russian history is the slow tempo of her development, with the economic backwardness, primitiveness of social forms and low level of culture resulting from it.
>
> The way out for it lies only in the victory of the proletariat of the advanced countries. Viewed from this standpoint, a national revolution is not a self-contained whole; it is only a link in the international chain. The international revolution constitutes a permanent process, despite temporary declines and ebbs.

He did not argue that every country would undergo revolution at exactly the same pace. Indeed, such a view he dismissed as naive. However, the international aspect was paramount. Even allowing for different speeds there could be no ultimate successful proletarian rising unless it was on a worldwide proletarian class basis. Applying his theory to Russia specifically, Trotsky argued that in accordance with 'the law of uneven development' the workers in that country, although relatively few in number and late to engage in the dialectical process, were the genuinely revolutionary force pushing both the bourgeoisie and the peasantry towards action. When the full revolution occurred, therefore, although the middle class might lead it temporarily, the industrial workers would then take over and press the permanent revolution to its pre-destined proletarian triumph.

> Within the limits of a revolution at the beginning of the twentieth century, which is also a bourgeois revolution in its immediate objective aims, there looms up a prospect of an inevitable, or at least possible, supremacy of the working class in the near future

Trotsky did not dispute that there would be set-backs along the path. Permanent revolution might well encompass periods of reaction and delay, but ultimate proletarian victory was assured.

> The political emancipation of Russia led by the working class will raise that class to a height as yet unknown, in history, will make it the initiator of the liquidation of world capitalism ... The Revolution, having begun as a bourgeois revolution as regards its first tasks, will soon call forth powerful class conflicts and will gain final victory only by transferring power to the only class capable of standing at the head of the oppressed masses, namely, to the proletariat.

Sceptics have argued that Trotsky, whose theory was very much akin to Lenin's 'telescoped revolution', which posited the compression of the bourgeois and proletarian phases into one, was simply forcing Marxist theory to fit Russian circumstances. In a sense this was the case, but it is not to say that either Trotsky or Lenin would have acknowledged any impropriety in this. Indeed, they saw it as their duty as true revolutionaries to interpret the Marxist message in the light of particular circumstances. What gave strength to this belief was that while Marx in his analysis of the class struggle had explained why it happened he had not described how it happened. As Robert Daniels, a noted modern authority on comparative revolutions, pertinently remarks: 'Marxism makes much of revolution as the transfer of power from one class to another, but devotes little theoretical attention to the way revolutions actually unfold'. The dialectic offered a convincing broad pattern but it did not provide the details. That was why Marxist revolutionaries, who were united in their belief in the dialectic as the dynamo of human history, were often widely and violently at variance over the question of how the dialectic actually operated.

TROTSKY, 1906–17

Writers on Trotsky have sometimes dismissed the years between the revolutions of 1905 and 1917 as being relatively unimportant, since this was the time when he and his fellow revolutionaries were detached from happenings in Russia and were therefore unable to influence the course of events. In one sense this was true. The various revolutionary parties do often present a comic spectacle, dashing from place to place, hounded by the police, and engaging in interminable argument often about the most abstruse points of order or procedure. Nevertheless, it was during this period that the Bolsheviks and Mensheviks hardened into distinct and opposed parties and the rival claimants among the SDs attempted to assert their authority.

For Trotsky it was a time of constant movement. With Natalya Sedova, whom he first met in 1907 and who was to remain his constant companion for the rest of his life, he set up home for varying periods in London, Paris, Vienna, Copenhagen, and New York. He poured out a constant stream of political works and also wrote widely on art and culture in terms of the revolution to come. He met all the leading international Marxists, and it is arguable that in this period he was more important than Lenin in the eyes of émigré revolutionaries. Despite his political activities, his group affiliation was difficult to determine. He was not numbered among the Bolsheviks, but neither were his Menshevik leanings very pronounced. He edited *Pravda* (the truth) and it was with some bitterness that he saw this journal taken over as a Bolshevik mouthpiece in 1912. It was this that prompted Trotsky to renew his attack upon Lenin for prolonging the split in the SD Party.

Lenin replied by referring to Trotsky variously as a 'careerist', an 'intriguer', and a 'Judushka', after a hypocritical character in a Russian novel. These were descriptions that would return to haunt Trotsky during the power struggle of the 1920s.

In 1913, Trotsky tried to re-unite the Mensheviks and Bolsheviks by forming the Mezhrayonstsy (United Social Democrats), but this movement made little headway and served only to make his exact political affiliation more difficult to determine. Despite their earlier differences, Lenin and Trotsky drew closer together over the European war that broke out in 1914. Both initially condemned it as an imperialist struggle and were dismayed by the willingness of the workers to fight patriotically. But both were quick to see that the strains and disruptions of a long war would greatly increases the chances of revolution breaking out in the warring nations. This duly happened in Russia in February 1917.

timeline	1907	begins his lifelong relationship with Natalya Sedova; has son by her
	1907–17	lives as émigré in Britain, Finland, France, Austria, Spain Switzerland, USA; prolific writer and editor of revolutionary works, including *Pravda*; becomes as outstanding a figure in international revolutionaries circles as Lenin
	1912	Mensheviks and Bolsheviks harden into two distinct parties
	1913	Trotsky tries to re-unite the Mensheviks and Bolsheviks by forming the Mezhrayonstsy (United Social Democrats)
	1914–17	Trotsky condemns the European war as a capitalist-imperialist struggle.

Points to consider

1) What is the function of the dialectic in the Marxist theory of revolution?
2) In what respects did Lenin and Plekhanov differ in their interpretation of the class struggle as it applied to Russia?
3) What influence did Trotsky's experience of the 1905 Revolution have on the development of his revolutionary ideas?
4) What did Trotsky mean by referring to Russia as being subject to 'the law of uneven development'?
5) How significant was the antipathy between Lenin and Trotsky prior to 1917?

TROTSKY AND THE RUSSIAN REVOLUTION OF 1917

THE FEBRUARY REVOLUTION

February 1917 witnessed the fall of tsardom and its replacement by the 'dual authority' of the Provisional Government, formed from the liberal parties in the last duma, and the Petrograd Soviet, recreated on the 1905 model. These dramatic changes had taken the émigré revolutionaries by surprise. As in 1905, they had been caught out by events. They rushed back to Petrograd, but it took most of them at least a month to reach the city. By the time the bulk of them had returned, developments had occurred which they had not directed. In the heady atmosphere that followed the abdication of the tsar, the tendency had been for thoughts of harmony between the parties to dominate. Since all the leaders of note were in exile, those Bolsheviks and Mensheviks already in Petrograd had acted on their own initiative. Believing that they were participants in a genuine revolution, they showed a willingness to co-operate with the liberal parties, from whom the members of the Provisional Government had been overwhelmingly drawn. The Soviet in its early weeks was genuinely representative of the factory workers and was not the Bolshevik-dominated body that it subsequently became. Initially it, too, was prepared to work with the Provisional Government.

LENIN'S APRIL THESES

Lenin changed all that. On his return in April, he berated those Bolsheviks who had followed compromise policies, and he denounced the Provisional Government as the tool of reaction. In his *April Theses*, Lenin exhorted Bolsheviks to abandon all thoughts of co-operation with other parties and to work for the overthrow of 'the present parliamentary-bourgeois republic'. He called for Russia's immediate withdrawal from the war, to which the Provisional Government had committed itself in order to receive loans from Russia's western allies. With the slogan 'All power to the Soviets', he expressed in pithy form his strategy for the Bolshevik infiltration and takeover of the Soviet as a base from which to seize power.

TROTSKY'S RETURN

Such was the political situation in Petrograd when Trotsky eventually arrived there from the USA in May, his return having been delayed by his detention in Canada on the orders of the British cabinet, responding to an appeal from the Provisional Government. He was carried shoulder-high from the train by cheering workers waving red banners. His reading of events soon put him in broad agreement with Lenin. His own theory of permanent revolution seemed wholly appropriate to the circumstances. The bourgeoisie had moved into power but were not prepared to undertake a full social revolution; therefore it required that the proletariat seize the initiative and drag the bourgeoisie in its wake, pending the outbreak of the international uprising that would guarantee the success of the Russian revolution. It appeared to Trotsky that 1917 was offering him the opportunity to turn theory into practice. This put him at variance with the Mensheviks whose prevailing view was that in the current situation Russia was not yet ready for a socialist revolution against the successful bourgeoisie.

By July, Trotsky had broken the last of the remaining links between himself and the Mensheviks, and stood fully committed to Lenin and the Bolsheviks. There were many in both the party he left and the one he joined who regarded Trotsky's change of affiliation as expedient and contemptible. In his defence, it could be argued that his becoming a Bolshevik was not simply a personal whim; it followed from the vote of the Mezhrayonstsy in July to merge with the Bolsheviks. It needs to be emphasised also that once he had made his change of party Trotsky wholly supported the plan for an armed insurrection against the

Provisional Government. The pressure of war and revolution in 1917 had brought Lenin and Trotsky together.

THE JULY DAYS

The month in which Trotsky joined Lenin and the Bolsheviks saw the fiasco of the 'July Days'. This was an abortive attempt by the Bolsheviks to lead a workers' uprising against the Provisional Government. The affair was confused, badly planned, and easily suppressed. The Bolsheviks had overestimated their own strength and the Government's weakness. Trotsky later claimed that it was a 'semi-insurrection', which the Bolsheviks had not organised but had supported out of solidarity with the workers. The rising was, in part, a reaction by some members of the revolutionary parties against their leaders' disinclination to challenge the Provisional Government. In one dramatic incident Trotsky physically intervened to save Victor Chernov, the SR leader, from being beaten to death by angry demonstrators. Following the collapse of the 'July Days' rising, Trotsky was arrested along with other prominent Bolsheviks. He had in fact invited arrest by writing openly to the Provisional Government, declaring that he stood wholly with the insurrectionists. This extraordinary step may well have been taken to convince the Bolsheviks that he was now truly one of them.

Many contemporaries were of the opinion that if the Government had acted with firm resolution at this stage it could have destroyed the Bolsheviks as a political force. But the Provisional Government, now under its third prime minister, Alexander Kerensky, a former SR, was more afraid of right-wing reaction than left-wing pressure and showed reluctance to enforce its authority. Trotsky and the others were soon released. If this lenient approach was intended to win over the revolutionary opposition it clearly failed. It gave heart to the Bolsheviks who tended to despise the Government for its weakness. Modern scholarship inclines to the view that Kerensky, in trying to hold an extremely difficult balance between left and right opinion, exaggerated the threat from the right. Judging that his government might be overcome in a direct confrontation with the conservatives and reactionaries he adopted a policy of conciliation towards the left. His essential aim was to placate the socialist parties and convince them that they need not fear that his government would become the agent of right-wing reaction. This is the most probable explanation for the strange set of events, known as the Kornilov affair.

THE KORNILOV AFFAIR

In August 1917, General Kornilov, Commander-in-Chief of the Russian armies, announced that he was about to march on Petrograd to prevent its falling into the hands of the socialists who were intent on betraying mother Russia to the German armies. Kerensky's exact position in all this has long been a matter of dispute. It used to be held that, faced with Kornilov's threatened attack, Kernesky colluded with him, then lost his nerve and called on the city to unite in resistance to the threatened attack. The view now favoured by most scholars is that Kerensky initiated the whole affair by first inviting Kornilov to bring his army to St Petersburg. He then turned on him and accused him of organising a counterrevolution. In Richard Pipes' words:

> All the available evidence ... points to a 'Kerensky plot' engineered to discredit the general as the ringleader of an imaginary but widely anticipated counterrevolution, the suppression of which would elevate the Prime Minister to a position of unrivaled popularity and power, enabling him to meet the growing threat from the Bolsheviks.

If that was Kerensky's intention, then he gravely miscalculated. His appeal to the people of Petrograd to rally to the defence of the city was promptly and eagerly answered by the Bolsheviks, who were thus able to pose as defenders of the government and the revolution. In a matter of days they had regained the prestige they had forfeited over the July Days. There was the further irony that the weapons that the Government had distributed to the defenders of the capital were never used since Kornilov called off his march. It was these same weapons that the Bolsheviks kept and turned against Kerensky's government in the October coup two months later.

TROTSKY'S STATURE IN 1917

Trotsky exploited the platform that the Kornilov affair had given the Bolsheviks. As if to prove the sincerity of his conversion to Bolshevism, Trotsky threw himself with enormous energy into the work of the Party. Sukhanov, a leading Menshevik, recorded that:

> He spoke everywhere simultaneously. Every worker and soldier at Petrograd knew him and listened to him. His influence on the masses and the leaders alike was overwhelming'.

He was certainly a far more public figure than Lenin, who, fearful of arrest, remained in disguise and made only irregular and fleeting appearances. An interesting observation on the respective contributions of Lenin and Trotsky came from the Bolshevik writer, Spunde:

> Trotsky displayed his best qualities in 1917. He was the idol of mass meetings in Petrograd; his political line aroused a great feeling for him . . .. Determination and boldness showed in everything he did. No one then noticed that he lacked Lenin's depth or Lenin's ability to subordinate all his personal feelings to the victory of socialism . . . Trotsky was one of the best orators of the revolution. He spoke everywhere with amazing brilliance and had the ability to popularize even difficult ideas with great skill.

The reward for Trotsky's endeavours was to be elected to the Central Committee of the Bolshevik Party. From there, in September, in what proved to be a crucially important move, he was appointed the leading Bolshevik representative in the Petrograd Soviet. The Soviet, which had come into being in March 1917 as a body broadly representative of all shades of progressive political opinion, had steadily moved towards the left as the year progressed. By September the Bolshevik members were in the majority; they immediately elected Trotsky as Chairman. From that point on, the Soviet was used by the Bolsheviks as a forum from which to attack the increasingly-reactionary Provisional Government for its outstanding failures, which they listed as its inability to create political stability, to lessen Russia's food shortages, to give the peasants land security, or to end the war with Germany. The Soviet was more than just a forum; Lenin had perceived as early as April that it provided the base from which the Bolsheviks could succeed to power. Aware of the fragility and novelty of party politics in Russia, Lenin calculated that it would be highly risky for a single party to attempt to seize power merely by its own authority and on its own behalf. If, however, the taking of power could be achieved in the name of the representative body of the proletariat this would cloak the nakedness of Bolshevik ambitions at the same time as it gave them validity.

Two critical factors need to be borne in mind when examining the events that led to the October coup: the continuing war with Germany and the fear on the part of the non-Bolshevik parties of a conservative backlash. The first factor suffused Russian politics and gave everything a transitory air; if the German armies were to break through and take Petrograd it would wipe out all that had been achieved since February. The second factor explained the willingness of the Mensheviks and liberal parties to maintain a common front with the Bolsheviks even when they disapproved of their policies and methods. In the uncertainty which prevailed in Petrograd during this period, the Provisional Government and its opponents both tended to overestimate each other's strength. This gave rise to political bluff and counter-bluff. Confusion and doubt became the dominant features of the time.

THE FORMATION OF THE MRC

There is observable, however, one clear-cut turning point. This was the formation in October of the Military Revolutionary Committee (MRC) of the Petrograd Soviet. Its creation was a response to the fear of imminent German attack. To safeguard the capital, it was agreed across the political spectrum that the city needed a special defence organisation. The original proposal for this had been a Menshevik not a Bolshevik move, but seeing a huge potential advantage to be gained from it the Bolsheviks were able to persuade, trick and cajole the other parties into accepting that the authority responsible for organising the defence should be a Soviet rather than a Government agency. The Bolshevik proposal that was finally accepted was that the MRC of the Soviet should be responsible for the protection of Petrograd, not only against the German armies but also against internal 'counter-revolutionaries'. Provisional Government blindness and Menshevik and SR terror of counter-revolution had unwittingly combined to allow the Bolsheviks to steal a march on their opponents, both on the left and on the right.

A montage of Stalin's victims drafted by Trotsky's supporters in 1938

Dominating the Soviet as they did and being thus in control of the MRC, the Bolsheviks had at their command a military organisation that was charged, as the successful resolution said, with

> ensuring both the revolutionary defence of Petrograd and the security of the people against the openly prepared assault of the military and civilian Kornilovites.

The Bolsheviks had thus acquired a military instrument with which they could directly challenge Kerensky's government. Trotsky later described this turn of events as a 'silent' revolution that gave the Bolsheviks 'three-quarters if not nine-tenths' of the ground they were to gain in their successful October coup.

TROTSKY AND THE OCTOBER REVOLUTION

Trotsky was the main Bolshevik organiser of events in the autumn of 1917. Yet it would be wrong to play down Lenin's role. He remained the great inspiration behind the revolution. It is appropriate to think of Lenin in the autumn of 1917 as the strategist and Trotsky as the tactician. It was Lenin who constantly pushed the Bolsheviks towards a seizure of power, refusing to modify his demands in the face of often quite cogent arguments in favour of delay or caution. With hindsight, we know that Lenin's strategy would prove to be a realistic and successful one, but before the event the Bolsheviks were deeply divided on the issue of insurrection against Kerensky's government. Some, such as Moishei Uritsky, were opposed to the idea completely, believing that they would be crushed, as in the July Days. Others, of whom Lev Kamenev and Grigor Zinoviev were the most prominent, while supportive of an eventual rising, believed that the time was not yet ripe since the party was not strong enough. Others thought that the Bolsheviks could not do it on their own and needed to act en bloc with all the socialist groups through the Soviet. Lenin accepted the necessity of acting through the Soviet but his constant insistence was that it must be a Bolshevik seizure of power. On this he would not compromise.

According to Trotsky's own account, Lenin had slipped back into Petrograd a few days before the critical resolution establishing the MRC was passed. At a dispute-ridden meeting of the 12-man Bolshevik Central Committee, held on 10 October, Lenin urged his colleagues to fix a date for armed insurrection. He was anxious that it happen before the Congress of the Soviets which was due to meet at the end of October and before the elections to the Constituent Assembly which had been arranged by the Provisional Government for November and December 1917. Trotsky showed complete loyalty to his leader in regard to the broad strategy. His only difference with Lenin was one of timing; he recommended that the rising be delayed for two weeks so that it would appear to be carried out at the behest of the Congress of Soviets. This was a compromise that Lenin appears reluctantly to have accepted.

During the next two weeks Petrograd was agog with rumours of an imminent Bolshevik attack upon the Government. The rumours were fanned by the public announcement by Kamenev and Zinoviev that they had resigned from the Central Committee rather than be implicated in an ill-timed and doomed insurrection. Trotsky did not regret that the Provisional Government should have been so clearly forewarned of Bolshevik intentions. Indeed, it was his aim to provoke Kerensky into action. What he wanted was that the Government should appear to have taken the initiative in trying to crush the Soviet and the Constituent Assembly. As he put it after the event:

> In essence, our strategy was offensive. We prepared to assault the government, but our agitation rested on the claim that the enemy was getting ready to disperse the Congress of Soviets and it was necessary mercilessly to repulse him.

One of the fears of those Bolsheviks who opposed a rising in 1917 was that they would not be able to muster enough public support. As it happened, that issue never arose. As Trotsky rightly judged, the task was not to gain widescale support for the Bolsheviks but to deny it to the Provisional Government. In the event, this did not prove difficult. The Government had not been genuinely popular since the first few honeymoon weeks of the February Revolution. As the year wore on, and it became evident that the Government was incapable of meeting Russia's needs, support for it evaporated. Its constant cabinet reshuffles did nothing to renew its efficiency or prevent its slide to the right. Although the Mensheviks and SRs exaggerated the degree of reaction that set in, it was clear that the Provisional Government had lost its progressive edge by the autumn of 1917. It was, of course, facing immense difficulties. As long as the war, to which it was committed, continued, it would never have the freedom, time or resources to begin the task of social and economic reconstruction expected of it. By October it was not so much a matter of who was prepared to fight against the Government as finding anybody who was willing to fight for it. As in any revolution, the vital question was the attitude of the military. Although on paper the forces of the Petrograd garrison were sufficient for the Government to meet any challenge to its authority, in practice very few of those forces felt any loyalty to the Provisional Government. Extraordinary though it seems, calculations suggest that in October 1917 scarcely 5 per cent of the Petrograd garrison of 160,000 were prepared actively to defend Kerensky's government.

The weakness of the Provisional Government was indicated by the ease with which the MRC asserted its authority over the Petrograd garrison. On 21 October Trotsky called together at Smolnyi, the Bolshevik headquarters, the representatives of the regional committees of the various military units that made up the Petrograd garrison. The representatives were then asked to vote in support of a Bolshevik motion, whose key passage read:

> Welcoming the formation of the MRC of the Petrograd Soviet of Workers' and Soldiers' Deputies, the Petrograd garrison pledges the committee full support in all its efforts to bring closer the front and rear in the interest of the Revolution.

The representatives were happy to approve this apparently innocuous resolution, which, the Bolsheviks, however, then interpreted as investing the MRC with the power to direct and command obedience from the officers of the Petrograd garrison. The few members of the garrison's military staff who subsequently refused to accept the orders of the MRC were branded as counter-revolutionaries. This Bolshevik manoeuvre had in effect begun the uprising against the Provisional Government. Without a shot being fired, the Government had been deprived of its military defenders. Kerensky failed to understand how defenceless his Government had been rendered until it was too late. When he did make a belated effort to summon loyal troops from the German front, the city had aleady fallen to the Bolsheviks.

Following these developments, the actual October Revolution was something of an anti-climax. As Trotsky had hoped all along, it was the Government that made the first move. On 24 October, it ordered the closing down of the *Pravda* offices and sent such troops as it could raise to guard the Winter Palace, the seat of government. The MRC responded by announcing that it was taking action in order to prevent counter-revolution. It disarmed the government guards outside the *Pravda* offices and sent them home, reconnected the telephones that had been cut, and re-opened the newspaper. MRC troops then occupied a number of strategic communication points, including the central post and telegraph offices, the main railway stations, and key bridges across the River Neva. By disconnecting the city's telephone system, the Bolsheviks effectively isolated the Provisional Government in its Winter Palace headquarters. None of these moves met armed resistance. By the evening of 24 October, Kerensky at last came to realise the seriousness of the position. He then contacted his commanders at the front, only to be told that they could offer no help. In frustration, he left the city the following morning, by courtesy of an official American Embassy car. His hopes of reaching the war front and returning with loyal troops came to nothing.

Lenin remained in hiding and disguise until the Provisional Government had collapsed. Trotsky, however, took great pains to keep him informed of what was going on. It was Lenin who drafted the offical MRC press statement of 25 October, declaring to the Russian people that the Provisional Government had been deposed and replaced by the Petrograd Soviet. Symbolically, it was the taking of the Winter Palace by the Bolshevik forces on the night of 25–26 October that marked the success of the 1917 Revolution. The event became the great set piece of Soviet tradition. But, in reality, by the time the Palace fell, the rising against the Provisional Government had already achieved its objective; Kerensky and his ministers had already fled. Moreover, the event lacked the dramatic character given it by legend. There was scarcely any fighting; the gates of the Palace did not need to be scaled since there were hardly any defenders. Bursts of fire from the building did occur in the early stages to delay the attackers, but these were infrequent and eventually stopped altogether when it became evident that resistance was pointless. The attackers simply walked in through the many doors of the building and disarmed the remaining and increasingly-reluctant guards. It is true that considerable damage was done to the building and its fittings, but this was caused by the looting that went on after the Palace had been taken.

The Congress of Soviets, whose opening had been delayed by the

Bolsheviks until the Winter Palace had fallen, began its first session in the early hours of 26 October. Trotsky, in language that was deliberately inflated in order to antagonise the non-Bolshevik delegates, described the Congress as 'the most democratic parliament in history'. The truth was, as he well knew, that it was a Bolshevik-dominated assembly, that did not genuinely represent the political balance of the Russian soviets. The Mensheviks and SRs made exactly this point; in a series of angry exchanges they disputed the right of the Bolshevik Party to speak for the Soviets, let alone the people of Russia. Rounding on them, Trotsky abused them in mixed metaphors, as being 'political bankrupts' who were fit only for the 'rubbish heap of history'. By the time Lenin entered the Congress on the evening of 26 October the majority of Mensheviks and SRs had registered their disgust by refusing to attend further sessions. To a rapturous response, Lenin announced three Decrees: on Peace, calling on all the warring nations to make an immediate 'democratic peace without annexations'; on Land, promising the transfer of State and Church properties to the peasants; on Government, formally announcing the list of Commissars of *Sovnarkom*, the new revolutionary government that was to serve until the Constituent Assembly had gathered. In historical terms, the three key names on the 15-man list were Lenin (Chairman), Trotsky (Commissar for Foreign Affairs) and Stalin (Commissar for Nationalities). The first stage of the Bolshevik seizure of power had been completed.

TROTSKY'S ROLE

In a later assessment, Trotsky attributed the Bolshevik success in October 1917 to three factors:

> the refusal of the Petrograd garrison to side with the government, the creation of the MRC, and the infiltration by Bolshevik commissars of the key divisions of the army. [These] completely isolated not only the general staff of the Petrograd zone, but also the government.

Trotsky was not being unduly modest when he commented:

> Had I not been present in 1917 in Petersburg, the October Revolution would still have taken place – *on the condition that Lenin*

was present and in command. If neither Lenin nor I had been present in Petersburg, there would have been no October Revolution: the leadership of the Bolshevik Party would have prevented it from occurring – of this I have not the slightest doubt!

This view neatly defined the indispensability of the two men to the successful achievement of the Bolshevik seizure of power. If Lenin was the architect of the Revolution, Trotsky was the master builder. Interestingly and ironically in view of their later relations, Stalin was unstinting in his tribute to the part played by Trotsky in 1917:

> The inspirer of the overturn from beginning to end was the Party's Central Committee headed by Comrade Lenin . . . The entire work of the practical organisation of the uprising was carried out under the immediate direction of the chairman of the Petrograd Soviet. One may state without hesitation that the party was indebted first and foremost to Comrade Trotsky for the garrison's prompt going over to the Soviet and for the able organisation of the work of the Military Revolutionary Committee.

The October Revolution had been a remarkably bloodless affair. But what lay ahead were three bitter years of violent struggle in which the Bolsheviks sought desperately to consolidate their hold on Russia.

timeline 1917	February Revolution – abdication of Tsar – the dual authority; Trotsky attempts to return to Russia from USA, but is held in Canada on British instructions; Lenin's *April Theses*; Trotsky eventually reaches Petrograd in May; joins Lenin and the Bolsheviks in July; takes part in the anti-government 'July Days' rising – is arrested, but later released; in September is elected as Chairman of Bolshevik-controlled Petrograd Soviet; MRC established in October; Trotsky organises the successful Bolshevik October coup against Kerensky's Provisional Government.

Points to consider

1) **Examine the political situation in Petrograd when Trotsky returned in May 1917.**
2) **Why did Trotsky join the Bolsheviks in July 1917?**
3) **How did Trotsky and the Bolsheviks turn the Kornilov Affair to their advantage?**
4) **How important a development was the creation of the MRC?**
5) **Trace the steps by which Trotsky plotted the overthrow of the Provisional Government in October 1917.**
6) **How accurate is it to describe Lenin as the strategist and Trotsky as the tactician of the October Revolution?**

TROTSKY AND THE CONSOLIDATION OF BOLSHEVIK POWER, 1917–20

Having attained power, Lenin and the Bolsheviks set themselves the task of destroying opposition in all its forms. This ruthlessness was the result of two factors. One was the situation in which the Bolsheviks found themselves after taking power. Indeed, the word power is misleading. They were a minority party whose grip on government did not really extend far beyond Petrograd and Moscow. They had inherited the same problems that had enfeebled the Provisional Government. The people were starving, and a huge part of western Russia was under advancing German occupation. There was little time for the niceties of democratic political debate and the development of representative government. It was a matter of sheer survival. The Bolsheviks' tenuous hold on power necessitated the most extreme measures.

But the circumstances were not the only reason for the Bolshevik attempt to assert total dominance. The second factor was ideological. Lenin and Trotsky now claimed that, as the vanguard of the international proletarian revolution that had begun in October 1917, the Bolsheviks had the historic duty of sweeping away the remnants of class opposition and reaction. Lenin's simple dialectical equation, 'who?, whom?', referred to the balance of political power at any given time. Who was exercising authority over whom? After the October Revolution the 'who' were the Bolsheviks, the 'whom' were those opposing them. It was the new Bolshevik government's task to crush the 'whom'.

This they immediately began to do: meetings of the Menshevik and SR parties were violently dispersed and their leaders thrown into prison. At a gathering of Bolsheviks in December 1917, some members of the Party expressed unease at the extreme measures with which the *Sovnarkom* had begun to enforce its control. Trotsky's reply perfectly exemplified his belief that in the revolutionary struggle ends justified means

> There is nothing immoral in the proletariat finishing off the dying class. This is its right. You are indignant at the petty terror which we direct against our class opponents. But be put on notice that in one month at most this terror will assume more frightful forms, on the model of the great revolutionaries of France. Our enemies will face not prison but the guillotine.

Trotsky doubtless had in mind the Cheka, which was established in December 1917 with the specific task of destroying 'counter-revolution and sabotage'. Within a very short time this special state police force, headed by the fanatical Felix Dzerzhinsky, had become a byword for systematic terror.

THE DISSOLUTION OF THE CONSTITUENT ASSEMBLY

The same ruthlessness which underlay the creation of the Cheka, was employed by Lenin to remove a major constitutional obstacle that threatened to bar the way to Bolshevik absolutism. In January 1918 the first meeting of the long-awaited Constituent Assembly was held; this body had been elected by some 42 million people throughout the whole of what had been imperial Russia. Since the February Revolution, the idea of the assembly as a democratic parliament representing the whole of Russia had been the dream of all the progressive parties. Even the Bolsheviks had accepted it. But now that they had taken power, they looked with suspicion upon a body which might well prove to be a limitation on their authority. Their suspicion proved to have been well founded when the results of the November election to the Assembly became known. The Bolsheviks had won only 24 per cent of the vote, giving them only 175 of the 717 seats. The SRs with 370 seats far outweighed them, and the other parties, Mensheviks, Kadets and the national minorities, could collectively outvote them. Lenin and Trotsky refused even to consider working with such a body. Asserting that the elections were fraudulent and that only the Bolshevik Party could genuinely represent the Russian proletarian revolution, they ordered its dispersal. The Constituent Assembly had sat for scarcely a day when it was broken up at rifle point by Bolshevik red guards. This blatant use of military force to destroy an elected parliament was the clearest sign yet that mere democracy would not be permitted to hinder the Bolshevik pursuit of total power. Some Bolsheviks and many foreign revolutionaries protested, but Lenin swept aside their objections. Trotsky noted approvingly that Lenin's revolutionary theories went 'hand in hand with the use of sharpshooters'. For Trotsky, oppression was justified by the needs of the class war; the immediate task was to humble the bourgeoisie:

> Until such time as they join the working class in the pursuit of a common goal, let every bourgeois house be marked as one in which so many families live who lead a parasitic mode of life, and we shall post yellow tickets on their houses.

Such unscrupulous policies naturally engendered bitter opposition and it was clear by early 1918 that the Bolsheviks would have to overcome serious urban and rural resistance before they could achieve complete domination of Russia. But before the Bolsheviks could attend to that domestic threat they faced an even greater immediate problem – the occupation of Russia by German forces.

THE TREATY OF BREST-LITOVSK, 1918

Although Russia had agreed to an almost immediate armistice with Germany after the October Revolution, the two countries were still technically at war. A peace settlement was vitally necessary if the Bolshevik government was to survive. As Lenin had often observed, no Russian regime could survive the type of crippling war in which the nation had been engaged for over three years.

It was, therefore, Trotsky's first major task as Foreign Commissar to negotiate a peace treaty with Germany. Here arose a conflict for him between theory and practicalities. As an international revolutionist, his expectation had always been that the outbreak of revolution in one country would precipitate international revolution; this was a major plank in his theory of permanent revolution. It had long been held by Marxists that Germany, because of its advanced capitalist character and politically-conscious proletariat, was the strongest candidate for revolution. Marxists had been disappointed by the readiness of the German workers in 1914 to enter enthusiastically into war rather than turn against their government. But Trotsky still maintained his belief that the strain of war would lead the German armies to desertion and revolution. Even while he was conducting peace negotiations with Germany he was encouraging Bolshevik agents to infiltrate the German armies and suborn the troops to mutiny. The German delegates' awareness of this added to the tensions of the negotiations held at Brest-Litovsk in occupied Poland.

Trotsky conducted the peace talks, which lasted from December 1917 to March 1918, against a background of considerable divisions among the Bolsheviks over the war issue. Lenin calculated that, since Russia was militarily incapable of continuing, an immediate peace was essential. Directly opposed to this were a number of Bolsheviks, known as 'Left Communists', of whom Nicholas Bukharin was the main spokesman, who urged passionately that the war should be continued and turned into a class struggle against bourgeois-imperialist Germany. Trotsky adopted an approach somewhere between these two arguments. As a realist, he knew that Russia was in no position to renew hostilities against the Austro-German armies. But, as an international revolutionary, he wanted the war to continue on both the eastern and western fronts in order to increase German exhaustion and thus create the conditions for revolution. The longer the Brest-Litovsk negotiations could be dragged out, the greater the chance of this occurring. In a number of votes in the Bolshevik Party Central Committee, Trotsky by a narrow margin over Lenin was able to gain acceptance of his 'no peace, no war' strategy.

Back at the conference table, he infuriated the German delegation by making propagandist speeches which never gave a straight answer as to Russian intentions. In exasperation, the Germans threatened to renew the fighting. Trotsky ignored a number of such ultimata until it became clear that the Germans would carry out their threat. By a single-vote margin, Lenin at last persuaded the Central Committee to accept the need for peace. On 3 March the Russian delegates formally signed a peace treaty with Germany. As much for international as for home consumption, Trotsky let it be known that the treaty was a German *Diktat* which Russia had signed under duress. The treaty deprived Russia of a million square-miles of territory, encompassing a population of over 40 million, and imposed large reparation payments on her. In answer to the anticipated condemnation of the Bolshevik readiness to sacrifice so much of Russia, Lenin made the riposte that within a year the treaty would be a dead letter, since Germany would lose the European war and so forfeit the gains of Brest-Litovsk. Events proved him right. When Germany collapsed on the western front in November 1918, Lenin's government immediately declared the treaty void and

Trotsky at Brest-Litovsk in 1918

reclaimed Russia's lost territories. A month earlier, Trotsky, aware of Germany's imminent defeat, had paid tribute to his leader's prescience:

> at the hour when many of us, including myself, were doubtful as to whether it was admissable for us to sign the Brest-Litovsk peace, only Comrade Lenin maintained stubbornly, with amazing foresight and against our opposition, that we had to go through with it to tide us over until the revolution of the world proletariat.

Trotsky's attempt to square the record could not hide the fact that both he and Lenin had gambled over the war or peace issue and had been saved by events. As for the onset of world revolution, this was wishful thinking. Whatever the German defeat may have presaged it was not the rising of the international proletariat. In any case, thoughts of engaging in revolution elsewhere had to be suspended as the Bolsheviks found themselves increasingly drawn into a civil war that threatened to destroy their grip on Russia.

TROTSKY AS WAR COMMISSAR

In March 1918, at Lenin's urgent request, Trotsky had exchanged the post of Foreign Commissar for that of War Commissar. Although he had no military experience and remained a civilian, he was told by Lenin that no other member of the Party could handle the task of saving Bolshevism. As War Commissar, Trotsky was now responsible for the defence of the Bolshevik Revolution against its domestic and foreign enemies. By a rapid twist of history, within 12 months of joining the Party in July 1917 Trotsky had moved from being an opponent of Bolshevism to being the director of its seizure of power and the organiser of its survival in civil war.

The war between the Reds (the Bolsheviks) and the Whites (a loose amalgam of anti-Bolshevik forces, including unrepentant tsarists, outraged liberals, embittered socialists and national separatists) was a desperate and vicious struggle. Complicated in detail, it was relatively simple in its underlying strategy. Essentially it was a matter of the Bolsheviks defending themselves on four shifting fronts against different White armies which, although supported at times by foreign interventionist forces, never acted in full unison and lacked the discipline and sheer determination to survive that characterised the Reds. Since the

A photomontage of Trotsky as War Commissar

war soon established itself as one of movement, Trotsky's basic strategy was to gain and keep control of the railway system. This would maintain the Reds' supply lines and prevent the Whites from concentrating their forces.

Trotsky's initial problem and eventual achievement was nothing less than to turn a ramshackle assortment of veterans and untrained recruits into an indomitable Red Army of some three million troops. By a mixture of bribery and threats (he was not above taking family hostages in order to enforce compliance), he recommissioned thousands of former tsarist officers to train and command the new army. Realism told him that was the only solution given the pressure of time and circumstances. To quieten the ideological objections of a number of Bolsheviks and to ensure loyalty from the officers, Trotsky attached political commissars to each army unit; their function was to keep a constant watch on the military and political behaviour of the officers. The commissars were hated by the army, but they performed their spying role with such zeal that Trotsky later employed the same system in the factories when he became responsible for labour output.

The commissars were one aspect of the severe discipline and centralised control that Trotsky imposed. Soldiers' committees which had come into being after the February Revolution were no longer permitted and the hierarchy of army ranks was restored. Volunteers did come forward to form the elite units, but the greater part of the three million recruits were conscripted. Desertion was made a capital offence, and the same penalty was meted out for serious insubordination or failure to carry out central orders. In Trotsky's words, 'Masses of men cannot be led towards death unless the army command has the death penalty in its arsenal'. Those who could not fight or who were deemed too unreliable to serve at the front were forced into non-combative labour battalions. To provide support services, skilled professionals, especially medical staff and engineers, were put under military discipline so as to enforce their compliance. People living in Bolshevik-held regions were required to contribute food and resources to the war effort. Grain requisitioning was enforced in the countryside. Those thought guilty of waste or black-market speculation could expect a savage beating at best, summary execution at worst. The Reds justified such severity by the cry 'Everything for the Front'. It should also be noted that Trotsky was able to tap a genuine enthusiasm among some sections of the population. The belief in a brave new world, first engendered by the February Revolution, had survived the October coup and still inspired many into thinking they were fighting a worthy cause. Trotsky showed great shrewdness in playing upon such emotions. The following is typical of the tone of the constant stream of rallying orders that he issued:

> Comrade Communists of the Third Army! It is up to you to save the revolutionary honour of the Third Army and, along with that, to save the Revolution. In the situation which has been created for the Third Army and for the country, communists cannot have doubts or hesitations; there can be no going back, no indulgence in criticism, but one slogan only: Forward!

Trotsky showed equal soundness of judgement as a political agitator. Under him, the Reds won the propaganda war in the countryside. They played upon the peasants' direct experience of White brutality to convince them that whatever the current shortcomings of Bolshevik rule, the victory of the White reactionaries would spell disaster and misery for the peasantry.

One of the most remarkable features of Trotsky's activity as War Commissar was the use of his own special train, by means of which he maintained constant and direct contact with the front. The train was more than just a vehicle; it was a town on wheels. It served as administrative centre, command post, military headquarters, arsenal, supply centre, troop transporter, publishing house, radio station, garage and work-shop, education centre, court martial, and rallying point. Its very presence in a particular area was enough to inspire the Reds and terrify the Whites. During the civil war, Trotsky's train travelled some 70,000 miles along the various fronts. The following is a calculation by the Russian historian, N.S.Tarkhova, of the train's itinery:

> 1918 – the Eastern Front: Sviyazhsk, Kazan; the Southern Front: Kozlov, Liski, Bobrov, Voronezh, Tambov Province.
> 1919 – the Southern Front: Kursk, Valuiki, Balashov; the Petrograd Front: Yamburg; the Eastern Front: Samara, Penza, Simbirsk, Kazan, Vologda, Vyatka; the Southern Front: Kjozlov, Kupyansk, Izyum, Boguchar, Kharkov, Lozovaya, Kremenchug, Mirgorod, Konotop, Tula, Orel; the Western Front: Petrograd.
> 1920 – the Eastern Front: Samara, Ekaterinburg; the Western

Front: Smolensk, Zhlobin, Mogilev; the Southern Front: Kharkov. Of course, this is not a complete record of towns visited; those listed are the major milestones on the train's journey . . .

As Trotsky himself put it:

> For two and half years, except for comparatively short intervals, I lived in a railway-coach . . . There I received those who brought reports, held conferences with local military and civil authorities, studied telegraphic despatches, dictated orders and articles. From it I made long trips along the front in automobiles with my co-workers.

Trotsky's description of how the train was used serves as a definition of his own role as Red Army commander: 'The train linked the front with the base, solved urgent problems on the spot, educated, appealed, supplied, rewarded and punished'.

A number of commentators have suggested that the importance of Trotsky as War Commissar had been overstated. They challenge whether he ever showed any real military skills, and suggest that most of the key decisions during the civil war were taken by the Central Committee. The historian and Soviet general, Dimitri Volkogonov, dismisses Trotsky as a 'dilettante' in military affairs. However, it is important not to judge Trotsky by the wrong criteria. He never claimed to be a soldier; he saw his essential task as being to inspire and, where necessary, to terrorise the Reds into victory. As Roy Medvedev puts it: 'Trotsky did not aim to become a military leader in the strict sense of the word. He remained a civilian. He was in fact the People's Commissar, not the commander of the Red Army'.

Moreover, whatever Trotsky's limitations as a strategist may have been, they did not greatly matter when set against the combination of energy, ferocity, and dedication that he brought to his task. Actions speak louder than words. Whatever his detractors may have said, the fact remains that the Reds won the civil war. They showed themselves more ruthless, more committed, and, despite the coercion to which they were subjected, of higher morale than the Whites. These attributes were in no small measure the result of example they were set from the top. The idea that Trotsky's leadership of the Red Army represents the third major achievement of his career still holds firm.

`timeline`	1917	Trotsky appointed Commissar for Foreign Affairs
		creation of the Cheka
	1918	dissolution of the Constituent Assembly
		Trotsky negotiates Brest-Litovsk Treaty with Germany
		becomes War Commissar
	1918-20	organises Red Army that defeats the Whites in the civil war

Points to consider

1) How did Trotsky justify the dissolution of the Constituent Assembly in 1918?
2) By what methods did Trotsky fashion an effective Red Army?
3) Of what special significance was 'Trotsky's train'?
4) Consider Volkogonov's charge that Trotsky was a 'dilettante' in military matters.

7

TROTSKY AND LENIN, 1920–3

Even as Trotsky was leading the Bolsheviks to victory in the civil war, he was having to contend with political challenge. Red commanders at the front often resented taking orders from a civilian War Minister. As for the local commissars, they were frequently ambitious men, keen to promote themselves politically, even if this meant challenging Trotsky's instructions. The most notorious clash was Trotsky's confrontation with Stalin, who was serving as political commissar in the Caucasus. Trotsky had to pull rank in order to force Stalin to desist from interfering in military operations. This incident is usually regarded as marking the beginning of their personal rivalry.

WAR COMMUNISM

War communism, the term used to denote the hardline policies adopted by the Bolsheviks during the civil war, was particularly identified with Trotsky. Although ruthlessness was a fundamental feature of the Bolshevik approach to the problem of establishing its authority, if such severity aroused more opposition than it crushed, it could leave its advocates in a weaker position within the party. It is another of the odd features about Trotsky that his words and actions very quickly became common knowledge, whereas Lenin and Stalin often achieved their ends surreptitiously.

By late 1919, as it became clear to Trotsky that the Reds were winning the civil war, his thoughts turned increasingly to the question of how the economic recovery which Soviet Russia so desperately needed could be organised. The success achieved militarily by the rigid methods of war communism led him to conclude that the same pattern of stern, centrally-directed, compulsion was the best means of inaugurating industrial expansion. He circulated his ideas privately to members of the Central Committee. However, within a short time they had been leaked to a wide audience as 'Trotsky's theses'. Thereafter he was generally regarded as the most uncompromising of hard-line Bolsheviks.

Early in 1920, he told the All-Russian Conference of Trade Unions that they were full of 'unnecessary chatterboxes' and needed 'shaking up'. He defended the principle of bringing industry under martial discipline and proposed that the workers be represented by a government agency rather than independent unions.

> The working classes cannot be nomads. They must be commanded just like soldiers. That is the basis of the militarisation of labour, and without it, there can be no serious talk of industrialising on new foundations.

Trotsky in 1920

When informed of this destruction of the trade unions as a separate force, Lenin expressed reservations. This appeared to put Trotsky at variance with his leader, and some of his opponents, notably Kamenev, Zinoviev and Tomsky, the trade union leader, tried to make much of it. But it has to be said that Trotsky's plans were perfectly in line with Lenin's basic policies. Consistently since 1917 Lenin had been working towards a one-party state and a centrally-controlled economy. The outlawing of the SRs and the Mensheviks, the main supporters of the trade unions, and the creation of *Vesenkha*, the Supreme Council of the National Economy, were the outstanding examples of this. Yet those Bolsheviks who were unhappy with this destruction of any vestige of democracy and at these centralising tendencies directed their criticism not at Lenin but at Trotsky.

THE KRONSTADT RISING, 1921

Those who wished to attack Trotsky for the severity of his policies under war communism were given powerful ammunition by his handling of the Kronstadt Rising in 1921. In March of that year, the workers and sailors at the Kronstadt naval base, 15 miles outside Petrograd, came out in a mass demonstration against the privations imposed on the Russian people by war communism. There had been similar protests elsewhere. What made Kronstadt special was that the protesters had all been Bolshevik supporters. Trotsky had earlier described the sailors of Kronstadt as the 'heroes of the Revolution'. Now here they were protesting against the failure of the Bolshevik government to live up to its revolutionary promise. Their manifesto began:

> In carrying out the October Revolution, the working class hoped to achieve its liberation. The outcome has been even greater enslavement. Power has passed from a monarchy into the hands of usurpers.

The demands of the protesters included the restoration of free speech and trade union rights, the end of the militarisation of labour, the stopping of special food rations and privileges for Bolsheviks, and the recognition of the right of other socialist parties to exist. This list was very much a condemnation of all the major policies followed by Trotsky and Lenin since 1917. This challenge to the Bolshevik authority was embarrassing and unacceptable. Trotsky, acting on Lenin's orders crushed the rising with the utmost severity. Some 50,000 Red Army troops, under the command of General Tukhachevsky, eventually overwhelmed the 14,000 armed defenders, but only after days of ferocious resistance. Savage reprisals followed. Trotsky's official propaganda branded the Kronstadt as rebels in the pay of the Whites, but the truth was that this had been a spontaneous anti-Bolshevik rising.

NEP AND FACTIONALISM

Lenin saw the light. At the meeting of the tenth Party Congress which coincided with the suppression of the Kronstadt Rising, he announced the introduction of the New Economic Policy. The essence of this new departure was that a limited amount of capitalism would be allowed to operate in Russia. State grain requisitioning would cease, and the peasants would be permitted to hold markets and trade for a cash profit. Lenin emphasised that the sole reason for this adjustment was the desperate need for food; Russia was in the grip of famine. Notwithstanding its military achievements, war communism was manifestly not producing the necessary resources to feed the people. A temporary return to more traditional methods on the land was expected to make up the agricultural short fall. To stress that NEP was not in any way a weakening of communist resolve, Lenin accompanied its introduction with the announcement of even tighter controls to be exercised by the government over industry and on the political front. One aspect of this was his prohibition on what he termed party 'factionalism'. Lenin requested and gained massive support for his proposal that:

> The Congress orders the immediate dissolution, without exception, of all groups that have been formed on the basis of some platform or other, and instructs all organisations to be very strict in ensuring that no manifestations of factionalism of any sort be tolerated.

Lenin's motive was twofold: to crush the 'Workers' Opposition' group within the Bolshevik Party, which had protested against the excesses of war communism and had been implicated in the Kronstadt Rising, and to pre-empt open criticism of NEP. The denunciation of factionalism had far-reaching consequences for the CPSU and for Trotsky. It could not, of course, prevent differences of opinion developing, but what it did was to stifle genuine criticism of leaders or party policy. If someone, such as Trotsky, were to find himself isolated or in an obvious minority, any protest he might make could be branded as disloyalty to the party. Any leader who might emerge after Lenin would be in a position to use the embargo on factionalism to destroy opposition. The ban was not officially aimed at Trotsky. Indeed, at the Congress Trotsky welcomed the proposal and called on delegates not to engage in self-wounding debate about the question of trade union rights. Nevertheless, given the widely-held view among party members that Trotsky was an outsider, his position in the party had been considerably weakened by the resolutions of the tenth Congress.

How much so became apparent in the developments that occurred between the Congress in 1921 and Lenin's death three years later. Lenin's progressive illness which became particularly marked from 1921 onwards meant that although he nominally remained in control of affairs he was often absent from the political centre for long periods. By 1922 a 'troika' of Kamenev, Zinoviev and Stalin had in effect taken over the everyday work and decision making of the government. This was never formally acknowledged or claimed, but it became a reality nonetheless. Trotsky tried to counter this by drawing the attention of the ailing Lenin to the growth of 'bureaucratism' in the party. According to Trotsky's own later account, Lenin was on the verge of co-operating with him to block this development when he was incapacitated by his severest stroke in March 1923. This left Trotsky isolated among the caucuses that were forming at the top of the party.

As to Trotsky's views on NEP, these have long been a matter of dispute between his supporters and detractors. Some argue that Trotsky had already moved towards NEP a year before it was formally introduced by Lenin in 1921, and so was easily able to adapt to it. Others assert that despite his public acceptance of it at the tenth Party Congress, Trotsky remained an implacable opponent of any deviation from hard-line socialism. What can be said clearly is that NEP necessarily involved all the Bolsheviks in contradiction. As Lenin admitted, although he attempted to depict it as only a temporary phase, NEP was a reversion to capitalism. This was clear evidence that socialism did not have the answer to Russia's economic supply problems. Trotsky, like Lenin, had to make the best of a situation which had not developed in accordance with expectation and political theory.

He took consolation from the fact that NEP was intended only as an interim measure. He referred to it as belonging to 'the transition epoch' when the planned economy could work in co-operation with the market. He developed this notion in *The New Course*, a series of articles, which he wrote in 1923:

> For the next period, which is what interests us practically, we shall have a planned state economy, allying itself more and more with the peasant market and, as a result, adapting itself to the latter in the course of its growth.

FOREIGN AFFAIRS

Trotsky's adaptation to NEP is of a piece with his adjustments in regard to foreign policy. His earlier expectations of world revolution following rapidly in the wake of October 1917 had not materialised. Trotsky interpreted this as a matter of altered timing not as a failure of his concept of permanent revolution. He had been fully supportive of the Bolshevik invasion of Poland in 1920. Like Lenin, he had expected that the Polish workers would welcome the Red army as class liberators; instead, the Poles fiercely and successfully resisted them as Russian aggressors. This was clear proof that the international revolution was not going to occur, at least in the immediate future. Trotsky did not despair; he had never claimed that the revolution would be a single happening. Indeed, his argument was that it was a process not an event. Given the complexity of the class structure and its uneven development within different regions and different countries, the revolution, though relentless in its underlying dynamic, would often be a halting affair as the dispossessed classes fought their rearguard action. 'Two steps forward, one step backward' was how Trotsky defined revolutionary advance.

The same hard-headedness attached to Trotsky's initiative in achieving the Treaty of Rapallo between Soviet Russia and Germany in 1922. Shunned by the rest of Europe as the 'pariah nations', Russia and Germany had good reason for drawing closer together. Each could offer the other commerical and diplomatic returns not available elsewhere. Trotsky was prepared to overlook the obvious fact that as an advanced bourgeois nation Germany was an ideological enemy. The trading and financial advantages that the Treaty brought an economically-straitened Russia far outweighed any theoretical considerations. For Trotsky this was simply a further illustration of the compromises that the law of uneven development imposed on practising revolutionaries.

THE SCISSORS CRISIS

Critics were quick to question Trotsky's commitment to NEP late in 1923 when a dispute arose within government and party over the 'Scissors Crisis'. The term referred to the widening gap that had opened under NEP between agricultural and industrial prices. The simplest explanation for the phenomenon was that agriculture had been successful and industry had not, with the result that agricultural prices fell because of a glut of produce while the cost of industrial goods rose because of their scarcity. The effect of this disparity, which Trotsky compared figuratively to the open blades of a pair of scissors, was that the peasants, obliged to sell their produce at minimum profit, were unable to afford the increased cost of manufactured goods. This recreated precisely the same problem that NEP had been designed to solve – without a cash incentive the peasants would return to subsistence farming and cease producing surplus food.

The Central Committee created a special 'Scissors Committee' to examine the problem. Declining to sit on the Committee, Trotsky led a group of party members, known from their number as 'the Platform of 46', in openly criticising *Gosplan* (the former *Vesenkha*) for its 'flagrant radical errors of economic policy'. Trotsky's charge was that the goverment had placed the interests of the *Nepmen* (the NEP profiteers) above those of the Revolution and the Russian people. He urged a return to a much tighter state control of industry, and warned that under NEP:

> The internal social contradictions of the revolution which were automatically compressed under War Communism . . . unfold unfailingly and seek to find political expression.

What prevented a serious split occurring in the party at this juncture was an industrial resurgence that had the effect of closing the blades of the scissors. By early 1924, industrial production had regained the pre-NEP levels of 1921. Nevertheless, the crisis had again revealed Trotsky's far from secure position in the Bolshevik hierarchy. The Platform of 46 was interpreted by critics as Trotsky's attempt to form a base from which he intended not only to attack Lenin's NEP but also to advance his 'Bonapartist' claims to leadership of the Party. Again the image was presented of Trotsky the outsider.

TROTSKY AND LENIN

It would be appropriate to refer to Trotsky as a Bolshevik scapegoat. But it also has to be said that he was a willing one. His loyalty to Lenin made him prepared to suffer the criticism of his fellow Bolsheviks. Such forbearance sprang not from humility but its opposite. He gave the impression of regarding himself as being above his fellows. There was also the fact of Lenin's recognition of Trotsky's worth. As long as Lenin remained in control of affairs, Trotsky did not need a bloc of supporters within the party; but, once Lenin's direct influence was removed, as it would be from 1923 after his final crippling stroke, Trotsky's isolation would be all too apparent. He would be blamed for having done those things which all along had been part of Lenin's programme for imposing the Party's absolute authority on the nation.

In his Menshevik period, Trotsky had consistently attacked Bolshevism for its centralist tendencies and Lenin for investing the party with too much importance in the revolutionary process. Yet as a member of Lenin's Bolshevik government after 1917, Trotsky did more than any other member to centralise power in the state and to make Lenin's party the source of absolute authority. Trotsky had co-operated with Lenin in all the main stages of the imposition of Bolshevik dominance. The crushing of the Mensheviks had been a double blow against opposition, since they had been the major defenders of trade union freedoms. Lenin's condemnation of factionalism effectively ended genuine political debate within the Bolshevik Party itself. By 1921, the one-party state was in place. Throughout this process, Trotsky had been Lenin's willing lieutenant. He had completely withdrawn his earlier objections to Lenin's idea of the centralised all-powerful party and was now its principal advocate. In 1924 he made the following remarkable statement: 'My party – right or wrong. I know one cannot be right against the party for history has not created other ways for the realisation of what is right'. This was the same man who had written in his Menshevik days that Bolshevism was 'built on lying and falsification, and carries within itself the poisoned element of its own disintegration'.

timeline	1920	Red Army invades and is driven out of Poland
		Trotsky extends war communism to factories by militarisation of labour
		instrumental in imposing the 'Terror' on Bolshevik opponents
	1921	crushes the independent trade unions
		organises the suppression of the Kronstadt Rising
		at 10th CPSU Congress Lenin introduces NEP and ban on 'factionalism
		Trotsky accepts Lenin's NEP, but maintains hard political line
	1922	Russo-German Treaty of Rapallo
	1923	Lenin incapacitated by a stroke
		Trotsky's *New Course*
		Scissors Crisis
		Trotsky leads the 'Platform of 46' in criticising the government's handling of the economy.

Points to consider

1) Why was the Kronstadt Rising of 1921 regarded by the Bolshevik government as a particularly dangerous threat?
2) To what extent was NEP an abandonment of socialism?
3) In what ways did Lenin's ban on factionalism weaken Trotsky's political position?
4) Why was Trotsky prepared to see Soviet Russia enter into a formal treaty with Germany in 1922?
5) What economic and political issues underlay the Scissors Crisis of 1923?
6) How far was Trotsky responsible for the Soviet Union's being a one-party state by 1924?

8

TROTSKY AND STALIN, 1923–9

The struggle between Stalin and Trotsky in the 1920s is often presented as a titanic duel for power. While it is true that their conflict had a highly dramatic aspect, it would be imprecise simply to depict it as a personal contest for the leadership of the Soviet Union. Trotsky was reluctant to see it in these terms. Although after his exile in 1929, he made many attacks on Stalin as an individual, his main line was to condemn him as a representative of the bureaucracy that had taken over and distorted the Revolution. For him, the Trotsky-Stalin dispute was a personification of the deeper struggle between the genuinely proletarian revolution that he himself represented and the deadening bureaucratism that had usurped authority in the USSR following the death of Lenin.

STALIN'S STRENGTHS

In one sense it is misleading to speak of a power struggle in the 1920s, since with hindsight we know that the fight had been won and lost some time before Lenin's death. By 1924 Stalin had reached an unassailable position in the government and party. This had been largely accidental; it had certainly not been intended by Lenin and the other Bolsheviks, nor had it been planned by Stalin himself. The key to it lay in the inexperience of a revolutionary party which suddenly found itself in power in 1917 without having developed a systematic apparatus of goverment. The Bolsheviks' response had been to learn how to govern as they went along. One result was that the work of government tended increasingly to be exercised through committees, usually presided over by a secretary or commissar. A further effect was that government and party became fused, with a marked overlap of personnel between the Bolshevik Party's Central Committee and the government's Council of Ministers. In practice, the Politburo, the smaller inner cabinet of the Central Committee, became the most powerful body in the whole structure. Lenin had not been opposed to these developments. After all they fulfilled his aim, in which he had been aided and abetted by Trotsky, of imposing Bolshevik absolutism on post-revolutionary Russia. What neither of them had foreseen was the way the emerging pattern of Bolshevik rule would, by 1924, have provided Stalin with the means of achieving personal power.

At the time of Lenin's death in 1924, Stalin, as well as being in the Politburo, also held four vital posts to which he had been appointed between 1917 and 1922: Commissar for Nationalities, Liaison Officer between the Politburo and the Orgburo (the Party's organising body), Head of the Workers' Inspectorate, and General Secretary of the Communist (Bolshevik) Party. The combination of these offices made Stalin the indispensable link in the party and government network. His control over the party files meant he knew everybody, and that nothing could go on without his being aware of it. Moreover, he wielded the power of patronage; the key posts in the party were within his gift. The remarkable thing was that this accretion of authority had come about largely by default. Not realising the cumulative significance of the posts, the party had appointed Stalin to them because he seemed temperamentally suited to the routine and monotonous work that they entailed. Stalin, an opportunist rather than a planner, found power coming increasingly within his grasp.

TROTSKY'S WEAKNESSES

When it came to finding a successor to Lenin there was no formal open competition. No electoral system existed. Lenin, before his final illness, had intimated that some form of collective leadershhip should succeed him, but he had not had time to make arrangements. The bidding for power was, therefore, necessarily a matter of intrigue. In the race for the leadership Trotsky was his own handicapper. Earlier he had had a clear chance to promote himself, but had not taken it. At the end of the civil war in 1920, as Commissar for the army and for transport, he had been the head of the only two successful organisations in Bolshevik Russia. He had the support of the army, was in favour with Lenin, was a member of the Politburo, and was undoubtedly the party's leading theoretician. Despite his lack of esteem among the upper ranks of the party, he was arguably the most popular of the Bolshevik leaders among ordinary Russians. Yet he was never able to use these advantages to impose himself on the party or create a following that mattered. Such supporters as Trotsky gained did not include many in the upper echelons of the party. As Michael Reiman observes:

> Trotsky's misfortune . . . was that he, as representative of the left wing of Russian socialism, appeared on that wing when it was already occupied by Lenin and his supporters. Therefore Trotsky did not succeed in scraping together any sort of significant party or grouping. He relied on a relatively small circle of like-minded people yearning for a compromise between two basic tendencies within the Russian social-democratic movement – the Bolsheviks and Mensheviks.

Although Trotsky clearly perceived himself as the logical successor to Lenin, it cannot be said that his efforts matched his aspirations. It was during this period that Trotsky's recurrent mystery illnesses prevented his attending important meetings. He seemed reluctant or unable to exploit situations to his advantage. One such was the Georgian question. At the time that Lenin suffered his final stroke in March 1923, leaving him paralysed and unable to speak and write, his relations with Stalin were at a very low ebb. Although himself a Georgian, Stalin, as Commissar for Nationalities, had been very heavy-handed in dealings with the Georgian leaders. They complained strongly; Lenin took their side and sharply censured Stalin. He also wrote to Trotsky, detailing Stalin's mishandling of the issue. Strangely, Trotsky did not subsequently use this letter as a weapon against Stalin. It was also at this time that Stalin had quarrelled with Lenin's wife, Krupskaya. Convinced that Stalin had insulted her, Lenin demanded an apology. There is every reason to believe that had his stroke not intervened, Lenin would have demoted Stalin in the government hierarchy. Yet when Lenin died in January 1924 it was Stalin who was best positioned to succeed him. Trotsky's failure to take the opportunity to undermine his rival remains a puzzle. Leonard Schapiro observes: 'at the Twelfth Party Congress, in

1923, with Lenin's explosive note on the national question in his pocket, which could have blown Stalin out of the water, he remained silent'.

LENIN'S TESTAMENT

Instead, at that Congress Trotsky spent his time as the spokesman of the Platform of 46 attacking the government's mishandling of the economy. Since this gave the impression that he was opposing Lenin's NEP, it damaged him more than the government, and left Stalin unscathed. Trotsky displayed a similar reticence in declining to use Lenin's 'Testament' to embarrass Stalin. This was the only surviving document in which Lenin had set down his ideas on the succession. Written in December 1922, it was critical of a number of the leading Bolsheviks: the key passages read:

> Since he became General Secretary, Comrade Stalin has concentrated in his hands immeasurable power, and I am not sure that he will always know how to use that power with sufficient caution . . . Comrade Trotsky is distinguished not only by his outstanding qualities (personally he is the most capable man in the present Central Committee) but also by his excess of self-confidence and readiness to be carried away by the purely administrative side of affairs . . .
>
> the October episode involving Zinoviev and Kamenev was not, of course, accidental but . . . it ought not to be used against them, any more than the non-Bolshevism of Trotsky.

In a postscript, Lenin described Stalin as being 'too rude' and proposed that he be removed from his position as General Secretary. When this document came to the attention of the party in May 1924, Trotsky could have pressed for its publication as a way of destroying Stalin's claim to be Lenin's heir. Instead, having voted in the Politburo for its circulation, he then acquiesced in the Central Committee's decision to shelve the 'Testament' indefinitely. As it happened, the 'Testament' was made public a year later when it was published abroad by a group of foreign communists, who had obtained a copy from Krupskaya, Lenin's widow. Trotsky dismissed the document as 'a malicious invention, contrary to Lenin's real will and the interests of the party'

Some historians suggest that Trotsky's diffidence is explained by his fear that, with Lenin gone, the party could not afford to lose Stalin, who with all his faults, had become administratively indispensable. Support for this interpretation is provided in a strange way by Trotsky's prophesy in 1924 that Stalin would become 'the dictator of the USSR', a prediction that he justified in these terms:

> He [Stalin] is needed by all of them; by the tired radicals, by the bureaucrats, by the Nepmen, the upstarts, by all the worms that are crawling out of the upturned soil of the manured revolution. He knows how to meet them on their own ground, he speaks their language and he knows how to lead them. He has the deserved reputation of an old revolutionary. He has will and daring. Right now he is organising around himself the sneaks of the Party, the artful dodgers.

This was a bitter but strikingly-accurate analysis of how Stalin had made a large part of the party dependent on him. But logically such awareness on Trotsky's part should have made him more not less eager to prevent Stalin from stealing an advantage. It is difficult, for example, to understand why Trotsky did not appreciate the importance of appearances following Lenin's death in January 1924. He had been offered the opportunity of making the major speech at Lenin's funeral. But not only did he decline this, he also failed to attend the ceremomy itself. His excuse that Stalin had given him the wrong date simply is not true. The documentation shows that he knew of the real date early enough for him to have reached Moscow with time to spare. Instead he continued his planned journey and was on holiday on the day of the funeral. This was hardly the image of the dedicated Leninist.

THE STALIN-KAMENEV-ZINOVIEV BLOC, 1924–6

Looking back on the power struggle, it seems that there was an inevitability about Stalin's victory. After 1923 Trotsky was not administratively in a position to challenge Stalin. Although he was a member of the Politburo at the time of Lenin's death, he had failed to build a following such as that enjoyed by Stalin. More important still, when it came to conflict between the two, Stalin could always outmanoeuvre Trotsky by virtue of the key administrative positions he held. He could deliver the votes. At bottom, it was not a matter of

Trotsky's ideas being less attractive or his policies less workable; it was that Stalin, by the mid-1920s, was the essential party man. He had control over party membership; he could hire and fire; he could make it impossible for anyone to mount effective opposition. How deeply Stalin felt about affairs is not easy to judge, nor in the final analysis is it very important. Stalin owed his success not to his ideas, but to his tactical skills, skills which Trotsky never possessed.

The Stalin-Kamenev-Zinoviev triumvirate, first formed within the Politburo in 1922, continued to carry the fight to Trotsky. The prime mover in this was often Zinoviev, who was himself ambitious for power and had a particular dislike of Trotsky. An insight into the method by which Trotsky was isolated in the Politburo is provided by Balashov, a member of Stalin's Secretariat.

> Everyone was on the side of Zinoviev, who flung at Trotsky. 'Can't you see you're surrounded? Your tricks won't work, you're in the minority, on your own.' Trotsky was enraged, and Bukharin tried to calm things down. It was often the case that before a session [of the Politburo] Stalin would meet Kamenev and Zinoviev and agree a position. In the Secretariat we called these meetings of the troika the 'ring'. In the twenties Stalin always had two or three assistants . . . They all knew about Stalin's negative attitude to Trotsky and acted accordingly.

Despite such organised personal assaults, Trotsky tried to fight back. He sought to raise the argument to one of principle. He made a plea for a restoration of 'party democracy' and a restriction on bureaucratism in government and party. He complained particularly of the disappearance of genuine debate in the party and of the growth in the power of the Secretariat, which had begun to take decisions without consulting party members. Opponents countered by sneering that appeals for democracy came ill from the architect of war communism and the militarisation of labour. Undeterred, Trotsky continued to present his arguments in the meetings of the Central Committee and the Politburo and at Party Congresses. His most sustained attack on what he termed the 'anti-Leninist Right' was contained in his *Lessons of October* of 1924, in which he resurrected the memory of Kamanev's and Zinoviev's opposition to Lenin over the 1917 October rising. This was a dangerous game; pamphlets poured from the pens of Trotsky's critics pointing to his

Menshevik past and his many breaches with Lenin. The beneficiary of such Bolshevik infighting was Stalin. He watched proceedings with equanimity. It made his task of picking off his opponents that much easier.

By 1925 it seemed that Trotsky's position had become hopeless. Continually defeated in the major votes in the Politburo and Central Committee, his supporters were a diminishing band. Matters came to a head in the Party Congress of 1925. Zinoviev and Kamenev, Chairmen respectively of the Leningrad and Moscow Soviets, exerted their influence with the local party agencies to return a Congress that was heavily packed against Trotsky. The Congress duly voted for his removal as War Commissar. This humiliation might well have marked the end of Trotsky as an active Bolshevik politician. That he survived for another two years was due to a turn of events that suggested there was still some degree of fluidity in Soviet politics.

THE TROTSKY-KAMENEV-ZINOVIEV BLOC, 1926–7

Kamenev and Zinoviev, as spokesmen for the USSR's most developed industrial cities, had been persuaded that the slow progress of Soviet economy under NEP made the USSR highly vulnerable both to internal collapse and foreign invasion. They appealed for NEP to be abandoned and a return be made to enforced industrialisation. There was an obvious affinity between these proposals and the policies followed by Trotsky during the period of war communism and the militarisation of labour. Trotsky had thus been offered a political lifeline. In 1926 he joined his former opponents in the 'New Opposition'.

The evidence suggests that Stalin secretly welcomed the formation of this Trotsky-Kamenev-Zinoviev bloc. It gave him the chance he had been waiting for to rid himself not only of Trotsky but also of the other two members of the group whom he had come to regard as dangerous contenders in the leadership stakes. Stalin's command of the party machine and his ability to control the voting at crucial divisions meant that he was proof against any challenge. He turned to his supporters on the right who joined together in the Congress to outvote the 'New Opposition'. Kamenev and Zinoviev lost their positions as Soviet Chairmen, while Trotsky was voted off the Politburo and the Central Committee.

The original photo of Lenin, addressing a crowd in Moscow in May 1920, shows Trotsky and Kamenev on the steps of the podium. In Stalin's time the photo was either clipped or retouched so as to remove Trotsky

TROTSKY'S LAST YEARS IN THE USSR

Trotsky did not give up the struggle. He continued to protest as Stalin's grip tightened over the vestiges of opposition. Not unnaturally, a pessimistic note entered into his reading of the revolutionary process. He wrote that 'the hopes engendered by the revolution are always exaggerated', and likened the Russian Revolution to the first French Revolution, when a period of reaction had followed the first revolutionary stage. In a direct criticism of Stalin in 1927, Trotsky condemned him for abandoning the Communist Party in China in its desperate struggle with the reactionary Chinese Nationalists. He accused Stalin of forsaking the cause of the international proletariat and being the 'grave digger' of the Chinese revolution. This was a striking example of the clash between Trotsky's concept of permanent revolution, with its emphasis on international proletarian solidarity, and Stalin's advocacy of 'socialism in one country', the notion that the USSR's national interests always had primacy over international considerations.

Such attacks only hastened Stalin's resolve to remove Trotsky from the political scene. In 1927, at the Congress marking the tenth-anniversary of the October Revolution, Trotsky made what proved to be his last bid to attract enough votes to be be able to mount a challenge to Stalin's authority. The bid failed; his support had dwindled not grown. In retaliation, Stalin now proposed that Trotsky should be expelled from the Party. Congress voted overwhelmingly for this to be done. In January 1928, Trotsky was issued with an internal exile order and deported under escort to Alma-Ata in Turkestan, on the Soviet-Chinese border. While there he continued to agitate and tried to maintain contact with his opposition colleagues. A year later in 1929, agents of the GPU, the successor of the Cheka, handed him a formal document, charging him with 'counter-revolutionary activity'. The last sentence read: 'Citizen Trotsky, Lev Davidovich, to be deported from the territory of the USSR'. The process of turning Trotsky into a political non-person could be said to have begun.

timeline	1924	death of Lenin; the power struggle intensifies
	1924–6	Stalin, Zinoviev and Kamenev form a Politburo bloc against Trotsky
	1924	Trotsky fights back with *Lessons of October*, but lacking Stalin's power base, he is outmanoeuvred
	1925	Trotsky loses crucial vote in the Party Congress; dismissed from his post as War Commissar
	1926	joins with former opponents, Kamenev and Zinoviev, in 'New Opposition', but is again unable to match Stalin's control of the party machine
	1927–8	expelled from the Party and sentenced to internal exile in Alma Ata
	1929	banished from USSR

Points to consider

1) Why was Stalin so well positioned to bid for power after Lenin's death in 1924?

2) What were Trotsky's major disadvantages in his power struggle with Stalin?

3) Are there any logical explanations for Trotsky's disinclination to use all the means at his disposal to challenge Stalin?

4) In what sense was Trotsky using a double-edged weapon in his 1924 *Lessons of October*?

5) Did the 'New Opposition' ever have a realistic chance of successfully confronting Stalin?

TROTSKY IN EXILE, 1929–40

The last 11 years of Trotsky's life were spent in a variety of foreign countries. Since his status as a Soviet exile was a diplomatic embarrassment, none of the governments which granted him residence were happy with his presence. Living variously in Turkey, Norway, France, and finally Mexico, he continued his opposition to Stalinism. In lectures, articles and books, he sought to show that Stalin had usurped authority in the Soviet Union and had betrayed the Leninist Revolution by the imposition of a deadening bureaucracy. In 1938, from his residence in Mexico City, Trotsky helped establish the 'Fourth International'. This was intended as an organisation of workers representing the true socialist principles that he had advanced in his programme of 'permanent revolution'. The Fourth International stood in direct opposition to the Comintern, the Moscow-based organisation, which had been set up in 1919 as the agency of world revolution, but which had degenerated into the protector of Stalin's corrupted concept of 'socialism in one country'. Stalin's reaction to this challenge was to order his agents to remove Trotsky permanently. After one unsuccessful attempt, this was finally achieved in August 1940 when Ramon Mercader entered his home and killed him.

Despite Trotsky's assertion that the Fourth International was his greatest achievement, some historians question whether his life after 1929 was of any great value politically. He was detached from the centre of affairs, and circumstances made him an impotent onlooker, protesting against Stalinism but incapable of influencing it. Other writers emphasise that it was in exile that Trotsky fully realised his role as a revolutionary theorist. His prolific writings, shaped by his experience of actual revolution, were concerned with the study of the practicalities of the class war. Trotskyists argue that it was in his exile period that Trotsky brought together his mature reflections on revolution, which constitute the most illuminating and realistic interpretation of Marxism ever devised. One particular claim of note is that Trotsky's analysis of permanent revolution as it applied to non-European areas, such as China, created the political theory on which the anti-colonial freedom movements of the twentieth century were to be based.

It is now recognised that in the 1930s the USSR under Stalin suffered unprecedented political oppression and economic misery. But, at the time, offical Soviet propaganda declared that a new age of workers' freedom and prosperity had dawned. The USSR claimed that Stalin's policies of collectivisation of the land and state-directed industrialisation under the 'Five-Year Plans' were modernising Russia and making it proof against the economic ills afflicting the capitalist nations. Many liberal and socialist sympathisers in the West were ready to believe this, particularly since the western world was indeed undergoing a severe economic depression which could be interpreted as the 'crisis of capitalism' that Marx had foretold. Against this background, Trotsky's

Trotsky and Natalya in Mexico City in 1937

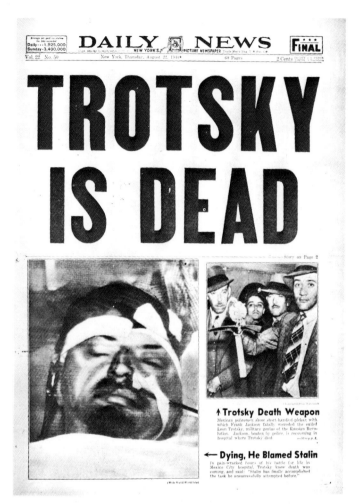

Headline from Daily News, *an American newspaper; August 1940*

criticisms of Stalin seemed like the ineffectual outpourings of the defeated. Moreover, Trotsky's castigation of the Soviet Union from afar was by no means unwelcome to Stalin. Trotsky in exile proved a very useful scapegoat for Soviet failures. Consistently throughout the 1930s, Trotskyism was used as a blanket term to cover all the counter-revolutionary evils which Stalin chose to identify and condemn. Those eliminated or imprisoned during the Stalinist purges were invariably accused of having engaged in Trotskyist plotting and sabotage. Since it had no precise meaning, the term 'Trotskyism' became a convenient synonym for everything corrupt and anti-Soviet.

SOCIALISM IN ONE COUNTRY

It is customary to describe the major differences between Stalin and Trotsky in terms of their respective slogans, 'Socialism in One Country' and 'Permanent Revolution'. Stalin's term, which he first used in 1924, referred to the belief that in the conditions of the 1920s and 1930s, with the USSR isolated in a hostile capitalist world, it made no sense to engage in a fruitless attempt to spearhead world revolution. That would have to wait. The USSR's primary task was to look inward and consolidate its own revolution by constructing a powerful industrial economy. In 1929, having overcome the protests of the 'right Communists', such as Bukharin, who believed in an evolutionary process involving the continuation of NEP, Stalin began the enforced collectivisation of the peasantry as a prelude to a massive industrialisation programme. Ironically such policies were not far removed from the war communism that Trotsky had practised; it would not be unfair to say Stalin's approach was a continuation and development of Trotsky's

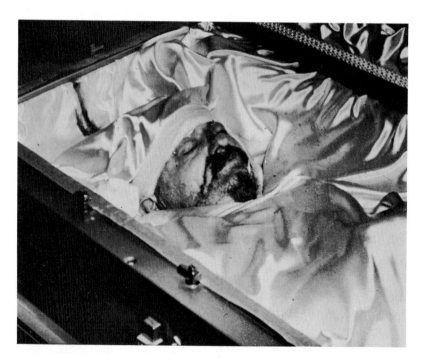

Trotsky lying-in-state

programme. Neither of them could, of course, admit this, but it is interesting that Trotsky in exile seldom attacked Stalin for the severity of his economic policies as such. Trotsky had never been against the idea of the planned economy. His charges were directed against the growth of the Stalinist bureaucracy which was destroying party democracy, and Stalin's refusal to acknowledge the needs of the international revolution.

Trotsky's celebrated attack on Soviet bureaucracy under Stalin needs to be seen in perspective. Trotsky never denied that bureaucracy was essential to the creation of a socialist society. His regimentation of labour and control over the trade unions during the period he was in power under Lenin involved the use of state power, which was necessarily bureaucratic. The throwaway line often attributed to him that after the October Revolution the Bolsheviks needed merely 'to pass a few decrees and then shut up shop' should not be taken too seriously. In any case, he was referring to foreign affairs rather than domestic policy. Although he believed in the revolutionary potential of the Russian workers as a class, he was under no illusions as to their social backwardness as a people; they required direction, and direction involves bureaucracy. Trotsky's complaints about the bureaucratic system as it developed under Stalin were much more particular. His concern was not for the Russian people, but the Bolshevik Party. It was Stalin's secretariat that he condemned for denying democracy to the Party members.

PERMANENT REVOLUTION

Trotsky's theory of permanent revolution was not new, of course. He had been developing it since 1906. Interestingly, the first use of the term was by Marx himself, and it is easy to see why committed revolutionaries argued so fiercely over the place it held in Marxist theory. It is also important to note that Trotsky was not against socialism in one country, if by that was meant the consolidation and success of revolution in Russia. But, as an international revolutionary, he could not accept that matters could end there. The very reason for consolidating revolution in Russia was so that it could serve as the inspiration and guide to revolution elsewhere. Nevertheless, in the tense atmosphere of the 1920s and 1930s Stalin was able to denounce Trotsky's advocacy of permanent revolution as proof that his opponent was an enemy of the USSR. It was suggested that, with world revolution not having occurred, Trotsky's interpretation made the USSR a hostage to fortune. If given free rein, Trotsky's intellectual fantasies would destroy the Soviet Union. It is fascinating to reflect that Stalin, the Georgian, was condemning Trotsky, the Ukrainian, for his disregard of Russian nationalism.

However, nowhere in Trotsky's writings is there the suggestion that the USSR should be sacrificed to some theoretical notion of world revolution. Trotsky's argument throughout was the very opposite; unless the USSR related itself to the international revolutionary process it could not survive.

> The way out lies only in the victory of the proletariat of the advanced countries. Viewed from this standpoint, a national revolution is not a self-contained whole; it is only a link in the international chain. The international revolution constitutes a permanent process, despite declines and ebbs.

In seeking to explain why the expected international revolution had not occurred in the wake of the October Revolution, Trotsky followed Lenin in scorning the proletarian leaders in other countries, who had pursued economism and amelioration rather than lead their class in the socialist struggle. It is interesting how Trotsky consistently thought in formulaic class terms. He was anxious not simply to condemn Stalin as an individual, but to define the errors of Stalinism in the context of the revolutionary process. Marxism was more than a political theory; it was a theology. For Trotsky, Stalin's greatest fault was not that he was an autocrat but that he was a heretic. 'Stalinism, wrote Trotsky, originated not as an organic outgrowth of Bolshevism but as a negation of Bolshevism consummated in blood'.

Russian Marxists continually drew on the French Revolution for historical parallels. The stages of revolution were invariably defined in terms of the French experience. The Jacobins were the Bolsheviks of their time, the Girondists were the reformers who stopped short of revolution, and Thermidor was the period of reaction that set in after the initial French Revolution. Trotsky specifically denied that the French model provided an exact blue-print for the revolutionary process itself, but he regularly used these terms in his own analyses. In the 1930s he pointedly referred to the dangers of Bonapartism, comparing the over-mighty Stalin to Napoleon Bonaparte, the all-powerful Emperor whose emergence had marked the final stage of the reaction against the French

Revolution. He spoke of Stalinism as 'inverted Kerenskyism on the road to Thermidor' and in a striking sentence he defined the Kremlin under Stalin as 'the Bonapartist bureaucracy of a degenerated workers state under conditions of imperialist encirclement'. In 1935, he explained the process by which Stalin had imposed himself on the Soviet Union.

> Stalin . . . is the living embodiment of a bureaucratic Thermidor. Today it is impossible to overlook [the fact] that in the Soviet revolution also a shift to the right took place a long time ago, a shift entirely analogous to Thermidor, although much slower in tempo, and more masked in form . . . The year 1924 – that was the beginning of the Soviet Thermidor.

While Trotsky, with understandable sensitivity given his own record, said comparatively little about the repression that accompanied collectivisation and industrialisation in Russia, he was swift to protest against the barbarities of Stalin's purges. He had strong personal as well as ideological reasons for so doing, since the members of his own family still in the USSR were cruelly victimised in this period. In 1939, he described the irrationality of the purges:

> During the last three years Stalin called all the companions of Lenin agents of Hitler. He exterminated the flower of the armed forces' commanders. He shot, discharged and deported about 300,000 officers – all under the same charge of being agents of Hitler or his allies. After having dismembered the Party and decapitated the army, now Stalin is openly posting his own candidacy for the role of . . . principal agent of Hitler.

INTERNATIONAL AFFAIRS

Trotsky's reference to Hitler raises the issue of the ambiguity of Soviet foreign policy in the 1930s. In theory, the Soviet Union was committed through the Comintern to aggressive Marxist expansionism. In practice, Stalin largely ignored this body and opted instead for an essentially defensive policy, aimed at protecting a vulnerable Soviet by a set of alliances. This approach was far from successful. France and Britain both rejected Stalin's overtures, and in 1938 those two powers joined with Nazi Germany and Fascist Italy in signing the Munich Agreement.

Traditionally, this Agreement has been viewed as the means by which the western European states appeased Germany over the question of German claims to Czechoslovakia. But to Soviet eyes it was an aggressive alliance of the capitalist nations against the Soviet Union. In desperation, Stalin ordered his foreign office to try to negotiate a pre-emptive treaty with Germany, which since the Nazi takeover in 1933 had conducted a virulent hate campaign against the USSR. His orders bore fruit. In August 1939 the two great ideological adversaries signed the Nazi-Soviet Non-Aggression Pact.

Trotsky in exile declared himself to be unsurprised by this turn of events; under Stalin the Soviet Union had shown a woeful ignorance of international socialism. He pointed out how Stalin's blind condemnation in the early 1930s of European socialist parties as 'social fascists' had prevented a broad Left alliance from being formed against Nazism. The bleak history of the Comintern confirmed this. Rather than being the vanguard of world revolution, it became simply a body for protecting the interests of the Stalinist regime. At its gatherings, the delegates from the foreign Communist parties were expected to take their orders from Moscow without challenge. It followed that, having failed to prevent the growth and spread of the extreme right in Europe, Stalin, fearful for Soviet survival, was forced to come to terms with the great ideological enemy. The result of this was the Nazi-Soviet Pact, the most glaring example of Stalin's abandonment of the international Communist revo-lution. Trotsky went further; he drew a direct link between the totalitarianism of Stalin's Russia and Hitler's Germany:

> the crushing of Soviet democracy by an all-powerful bureaucracy and the extermination of bourgeoisie democracy by fascism were produced by one and the same cause: the dilatoriness of the world proletariat in solving the problems set for it by history. Stalinism and fascism, in spite of a deep difference in social foundations, are symmetrical phenomena. In many of their features they show a deadly similarity.

In the period before the Nazi-Soviet Pact there had been suggestions by Trotsky's opponents that he was in fact anxious to see Stalin's Russia destroyed in war with Germany. Trotsky's answer is instructive.

> The USSR and Stalin are not the same thing. I am an adversary of Stalin but not of the USSR ... Hitler's victory would signify

frightful economic, political and national slavery for all the peoples of the USSR … To defend the nationalisation of the means of production realised by the October Revolution – against Hitler as against all other imperialists – I consider this the elementary duty of every socialist, beginning with myself.

Whether he would have honoured that last commitment cannot be known. By the time Hitler tore up the Nazi-Soviet Pact and unleashed Operation Barbarossa against the USSR in June 1941, Trotsky was ten months dead.

timeline	1929	Trotsky lives in Turkey
	1930–3	writes *Autobiography* and *History of the Russian Revolution*
	1933–5	lives in France
	1934	beginning of Stalin's Purges; Trotskyism used as a synonym for sabotage and anti-Soviet activities plotting
	1935–6	moves to Norway attacks Stalin's bureaucracy and betrayal of 1917 revolution
	1937	takes up asylum in Mexico City
	1938	helps establish the 'Fourth International', an organisation of workers abiding by his socialist principles of 'permanent revolution'; Stalin orders his agents to kill Trotsky
	1939	Trotsky condemns the Nazi-Soviet Pact as the logical progression of Stalin's betrayal of international revolution
	1940	Trotsky assassinated

Points to consider

1) Consider Trotsky's claim that the Fourth International was his greatest political achievement.
2) To what extent was Trotsky opposed to the principle of 'socialism in one country'?
3) In the 1930s, how far did Trotsky modify his theory of permanent revolution?
4) What did Trotsky mean by saying that Stalinism and fascism 'shared a deadly similarity'?

10

TROTSKY AND THE HISTORIANS

Trotsky was a giant, certainly a giant of the twentieth century. There have been other giants but Trotsky's situation was unique. Nobody of his stature has ever been reduced to zero in his own place, in his own nation, in his own culture. Stalin almost succeeded in wiping Trotsky out of history.

This passage by George Kline, an American analyst, refers to the remarkable situation in which for a quarter of a century Trotsky, having been defeated in the power struggle and driven into exile, was simply written out of the Soviet history books and treated as a 'non-person'. It was standard practice to erase Trotsky from photographs which might show him in a favourable light or even as having existed. It had not always been the case. In the first edition of the *Complete Works of Lenin*, officially published by the Soviet government in the 1920s under the editorship of Kamenev, Trotsky's role as revolutionary was fully acknowledged. Reference was made to 'his unique and now especially celebrated theory of "Permanent Revolution"' and his leadership of the St Petersburg Soviet in 1905. Significantly, he was credited with having 'organised and led the insurrection of October, 1917'. It was also recorded that he had been the victorious Commissar for War during the struggle against the Whites in the war of 1918-20.

The scale of Trotsky's achievements was unmatched by any other Bolshevik, with the possible exception of Lenin. Yet it was precisely their exceptional nature that prevented their being recognised once Trotsky had been exiled and disgraced. Trotsky's record was an embarrassment to Stalin. As a consequence, from the late 1920s onwards, Trotsky was treated in one of two ways: he was either totally ignored, to the extent of being wholly written out of Bolshevik histories of the revolution, or his name was used as the hated symbol of political heresy and anti-Soviet sabotage.

Given the situation within the USSR, the problem for non-Soviet historians wishing to study Trotsky has been that from the time of his expulsion from the Soviet Union in 1929 they had little access to Russian sources. Nonetheless, valuable studies did appear. In 1925 Max Eastman, an American communist and a major translator of Trotsky's works into English, wrote an informative description of the young Trotsky. Eastman had the advantage of having met Trotsky on personal terms in the early 1920s. He also had access to a largely hostile biography of Trotsky by G.A.Ziv, one of Trotsky's revolutionary companions during the pre-1905 years. Important details of Trotsky's younger days were also included in Victor Serge's, *The Life and Death of Leon Trotsky*, which was written in collaboration with Trotsky's wife, Natalia Sedova. It was Eastman who, prompted by the description of Trotsky that had appeared in the *Complete Works of Lenin*, suggested that the significance of Trotsky's career could be best judged in relation to three major achievements: his chairmanship of the St Petersburg Soviet in 1905, his organisation of the October Revolution in 1917, and his leadership of the Red Army in the civil war.

Although such books were published, and there were important collections of Trotsky's papers in Western archives, the wall of silence in Russia deterred most Western historians from attempting to study Trotsky in depth. His important role in the Bolshevik seizure of power was recognised and his writing in exile on Soviet affairs was given attention. But, as he was no longer at the centre of events after 1927, his views on developments under Stalin were usually judged as being the understandably-bitter reaction of a defeated opponent. Naturally, for active Trotskyists, rather than historians, he remained a living force. Trotsky was seen by them as the true revolutionary and genuine Leninist, whose leadership of the USSR had been usurped by the megalomaniacal Stalin.

Even after the onset of de-Stalinisation in 1956, begun by Khrushchev three years after Stalin's death, Trotsky was still not readmitted into official Soviet histories. The reason was that, despite Khrushchev's denunciation of Stalin for his crimes against the Party, there were too many Bolsheviks who, having risen to power under Stalin by doing his dirty work, were unwilling to see Trotsky's reputation restored at the risk of having light shed on their own behaviour. It is true that there was a considerable degree of historical revision during the period of de-Stalinisation, but the revisionists were still very circumspect. They were not entirely free to write objectively; their aim was to load the blame for Soviet failures on to Stalin while avoiding criticism of the Soviet system itself. Yet, even as late as 1987, in the time of *glasnost*, a notable Soviet historian, Yuri Afanasiev, was still repeating the Stalinist myth that Trotsky had opposed rather than organised the Bolshevik rising of October 1917.

A major exception to this play-safe approach was Roy Medvedev. A courageous dissident in the pre-Gorbachev era, Medvedev combined a deep commitment to the Soviet Union with a willingness to point out its past and present failings. His study of Stalinism, *Let History Judge*, first published in 1972, was not uncritical of Trotsky, but it challenged 'the obvious lies' spread over 50 years by Stalinists in the USSR and in the West.

Interestingly, it was a work not in Russian but in English that had quickened interest in Trotsky. In his research for a biography of Stalin, Isaac Deutscher became fascinated by the role of Stalin's arch-enemy; accordingly, he prepared a major study of Trotsky. By chance, the publication of Deutscher's work coincided with the de-Stalinisation process in the USSR. The three-volume book, *Trotsky: the Prophet Armed*, *the Prophet Unarmed* and *the Prophet Outcast*, published between 1954 and 1963, circulated widely, if unofficially, within the USSR. Deutscher had succeeded in making historians, inside the Soviet Union as well as outside, begin reappraising Trotsky's historical role. As the titles of the individual volumes suggested, Deutscher presented Trotsky as the prophet of revolution who had been rejected by his own people. Deutscher wrote, 'I see him as the representative figure of pre-Stalinist communism and the precursor of post-Stalinist communism'. The trilogy was soon acknowledged as the fullest and best informed biography of Trotsky up to that time. It was read widely if secretively in the USSR by a considerable number of scholars, who were greatly influenced by it even though they could not yet openly acknowledge it in their own writings.

Deutscher, in his book, did not attempt to hide Trotsky's weaknesses, but his own Menshevik sympathies tended to make his portrayal of

Trotsky basically an approving one. This did not in itself detract from the value of his study, but other authorities on Russian history, Alec Nove and John Erickson, for example, have doubted that Trotsky's career is of such outstanding significance. They suggest that it is Stalin who gives Trotsky such importance as he had by providing the great counterpoint. In the words of Terry Brotherstone, organiser of a ground-breaking international conference on Trotsky in 1990:

> there can be no meaningful definition of Trotsky which does not include the fact that the term came to take on a positive identity . . . only in opposition to Stalinism. It was the rise of Stalinism that created the necessity for something called 'Trotskyism'.

Few historians now deny that Trotsky played a critical part in the October Revolution in 1917, but there are a significant number who doubt whether Trotsky's life after 1927 was of particular value politically. Alec Nove asks: 'How important was Trotsky, after all? He had his brief glorious hours in and just after the Revolution, but he was speedily eased out of his seat of power and was increasingly ineffectual'. Other writers, however, lay stress upon Trotsky's contribution in this period to the theory of revolution. Sergei Kudriashov, one of the younger generation of Russian scholars, makes the remarkable suggestion that:

> if by Bolshevism we understand profession of the ideas of historical and dialectical materialism, struggle for the interests of the oppressed, devotion to the idea of proletarian revolution and dictatorship of the proletariat . . . then at the end of the 1930s, Trotsky was a greater Bolshevik than the whole of the CPSU.

Two biographers of Trotsky, Ronald Segal and Joel Carmichael, believe that Trotsky's writings amount to a unique and invaluable analysis of the nature and practice of revolution; no other participant in the Russian Revolution left such a legacy. Active Trotskyists, such as Robin Blackburn, go much further; they argue that it was in exile that Trotsky perfected his understanding of revolutionary theory, an understanding that made him the true heir to Marx and Lenin. Had it been Trotsky and not Stalin who won the power struggle of the 1920s, then the Russian Revolution would not have been diverted on to its fatal course. Trotsky's informed application of the true principles of the international proletarian revolution would have replaced Stalin's economically-disastrous pursuit of 'socialism in one country', and would have turned the USSR into the first truly socialist society. Such thinkers interpret the widescale collapse of socialist systems of government in the 1980s and 1990s as further reason for believing that if genuine socialism were ever to be re-established it could only be by means of applied Trotskyism.

This view is associated with the concept of the 'unfinished revolution', the theory that the truly-socialist workers' revolution which took place in 1917 had been subsequently betrayed by Lenin's successors. According to this line of thought, expressed by such writers as Deutscher and Adam Ulam, the gains made by the 1917 revolutionaries had been crushed by the repressive bureaucratic rule of the CPSU under Stalin and those who came after him. It may be said that events in Russia since 1989, involving the collapse of the Communist regime and the break up of the USSR, have made the notion of a 'finished' revolution even more remote.

Nevertheless, there are still Trotskyists who assert that all this is simply further proof of the inevitable disaster that Soviet Communism called down upon itself when it abandoned Trotsky and his ideas. There is also a strong school of thought, of which Udo Gehrmann is the leading example, which regards Trotsky as a more incisive political theorist than Lenin. Gehrmann views Trotsky's essentially realistic appreciation of revolution in action as being more in tune with practicalities than Lenin's *a priori* concepts derived from his reading of the French Revolution of 1789.

Committed Marxists have been understandably drawn to Trotsky. Given the horrors of Stalinism and the eventual disintegration of the USSR, those who still believe in the scientific truth of Marxism look to Trotsky, Stalin's victim, as the saviour of Marxist hopes. This viewpoint is very much an act of faith, since there is no way of knowing how Trotskyism would have fared in practice, but this in a paradoxical way gives greater conviction to those who believe in it.

However, it has to be said that Trotsky as saviour is not the prevailing view in the now dismembered USSR. Dimitri Volkogonov, who has emerged as a leading Soviet analyst, sees little difference between the two great rivals, Stalin and Trotsky. He even goes so far as to suggest that had the roles been reversed and Trotsky had won the power struggle he would have turned the world and not just the USSR into one great

Gulag-style prison camp. The Russian nationalist writer, Victor Belov, argues that the ferocious policies which Stalin imposed on the USSR after 1929 were extensions of those which Trotsky had first formulated. In a neatly-turned paradox, Belov suggests that 'Stalin was the chief Trotskyist'.

Such ideas are similar to those of Leonard Schapiro, an influential writer in the Western world, who had lived through the Stalinist years and whose personal experience of totalitarianism led him to suggest that it was Stalin's monstrousness that saved Trotsky's reputation. Schapiro's essential claim was that Trotsky's good name as a revolutionary rests upon a syllogism which runs as follows: Stalin was a tyrant; Trotsky opposed him; therefore Trotsky was opposed to tyranny. However, Schapiro's study of the record leads him to conclude:

> [I]f we take Trotsky's career while in power – not what he wrote or said about it in exile – there is nothing to choose between him and Stalin, or any reason to suppose that had he been victorious in the conflict, the Soviet regime would have turned out any better than it did. For they shared the same premise – monopoly of power for an all-powerful elite.

Arguably, the most authoritative modern study is *Trotsky*, written in the period of glasnost that preceded the break-up of the USSR, by the French scholar, Pierre Broué, Director of the Leon Trotsky Institute in Grenoble. What is of particular value in this study, published in 1988, is Broué's identification of the problem areas in Trotsky's career and the key questions that remain to be answered concerning his contribution to the theory and practice of revolution. It is Broué's contention that, while some of the answers can be gleaned from the various collections of Trotsky papers that already exist in the West, all the answers would be forthcoming if only the Soviet archives, particularly the KGB and Stalin collections, were to be opened, first to Russian and then to foreign scholars. Broué interprets Trotsky's place in history in accordance with his own strongly-Marxist views. Alec Nove speaks somewhat wryly of Broue as a 'true believer ... One of the keepers of the flame of Trotskyism'. This, it may be said, does not invalidate Broué's work, but, in the eyes of those scholars who have a less committed political approach, it makes his broader analysis questionable. One of the controversial aspects of Broué's book is that the writer tends to be dismissive of Deutscher's *Trotsky*. He challenges Deutscher's credentials as a historian, arguing that his sources were too limited, and that he 'covered gaps in information with his own imagination'.

A marked tendency among a number of modern historians is to refer to Trotsky as being a 'marginal' politician, that is someone who never fully belonged to the Party to whose cause he devoted so much time and energy. He was always on the fringe, never at the centre, even when he appeared to be directing events. Michael Reiman, a German scholar, suggests Trotsky was never a genuine Bolshevik and that the period of Trotsky's greatest achievements, 1917–21, was ironically one in which he acted out of character.

> in October 1917, it was Trotsky who to a great extent ensured that victory in the revolution belonged to a party which was not his own party and which he did not control. Apart from the initial period of the revolution and the Civil War, the only role open to him was as a critic of this party.

Trotsky's 'marginality' is a theme much taken up by Russian writers. Academician V. I. Buldakov, a distinguished analyst of modern revolutions, identifies Trotsky as being typical of so many of the *intelligentsia* in late imperial Russia who became revolutionaries. Trotsky's rejection of his Jewish race and family and his embracing of the 'people' was an example of the way alienated intellectuals abandoned reality for abstractions, to which they then became passionately committed. Buldakov quotes the view of Maxim Gorky, one of Trotsky's socialist contemporaries, that the *intelligentsia's* peculiar blend of dry intellectualism and passionate emotion led to a combination of 'social fanaticism and an extreme instability of democratic senti-ments'. Trotsky's Jewishness is certainly a factor that merits attention. He frequently apologised for his racial membership and it is significant that the reason he gave for not assuming Lenin's mantle was that his Jewishness would be an embarrassment to the government and the party. It may be that in emphasising this aspect ex-Soviet writers are deliberately isolating Trotsky and playing down his revolutionary con-tribution, but it has to be said that Trotsky has given them reason and justification for their viewpoint.

Such 'psycho-history' is perhaps a dangerous line of enquiry, but it is worth noting that Trotsky's personal history lends itself at many points to interesting psychological interpretations. Philip Pomper offers the view that Trotsky:

> showed the psychic wounds of a member of a victim minority, as well as those from his own personal development. The defence mechanisms he deployed against his negative identity and sense of imposturship clearly affected his political behaviour.

Certainly Trotsky's personality was in many respects an introspective one. His frequent illnesses appear to have been psychosomatic; he was scholarly and sensitive and could be moved emotionally by particular circumstances. Yet overall, certainly in his political career, he possessed an adamantine and ruthless quality, which enabled him to acquiesce in and direct the most unremitting repression of dissent.

By the middle 1990s, despite the end of what was formerly the USSR, Trotsky had still not been rehabilitated in Russia. The principal reason for this was that Trotsky was now interpreted along the lines of the left/right political divisions obtaining in the new Russia. The Left Democrats continued to view him as Stalin's precursor while the chauvinist right saw him as part of the Zionist conspiracy against Russia. It seems that, as during his lifetime, fierce controversy will always accompany evaluations of Trotsky and his place in history.

Points to consider

1) Have there been any significant changes in the attitude of Soviet and Russian historians towards Trotsky since the 1920s?
2) What difficulties have prevented western historians fully analysing Trotsky's career?
3) What have been the major divisions among historians over the issue of Trotsky's historical significance?
4) Identify the particular contributions made by Isaac Deutscher and Pierre Broué to Trotsky studies.
5) How effectively have historians treated the question of Trotsky's 'marginality'?

11

TROTSKY AND TROTSKYISM

Trotsky did not like the word Trotskyism applied to his political ideas. When he used it he always put in inverted commas. He claimed to be an interpreter of Marx, not the creator of a new political philosophy. He wished his role in history to be judged by how well he had understood and applied the scientific laws of revolution.

TROTSKY – SUCCESS OR FAILURE?

Trotsky's single greatest practical achievement remains his organisation of the October Revolution. He was the major executive figure. That Revolution would not have followed the course it did but for him. Lenin, as Trotsky acknowledged, was the great inspiration behind the Bolshevik coup but the actual organisation of the event was the work of Trotsky. His other actual achievements were also substantial. There is no reason to doubt that his Chairmanship of the St Petersburg Soviet in 1905 and his leadership of the Red Army in the civil war of 1918-20 were outstanding accomplishments.

But the Soviet system which Trotsky helped to create rejected him during the greater part of his life time, and then collapsed 50 years after his death. It was Stalin, not he, who wielded power for a quarter of a century. Trotskyism has the historical luxury of not having been put to the test. How logical Trotsky's theories were and how consistently he would have followed them over time can only be a matter of speculation, since after Lenin's death he was never in a position to put his ideas into practice. Since Trotsky held executive power for such a short time, being in government for only four of his forty-two years as a politician,

Trotskyists are thrown back on to the quality of his political theory as the justification for their belief in him. Yet here, too, his record is very limited. Trotskyism has survived into the world of ideas, but as a political movement it remains very much a minority, fringe, activity. The Fourth International by which Trotsky put such great store won devotees in some 30 countries but then broke up into competing factions. Never being remotely in a position to put its ideas into operation, it has remained a historical curiosity.

In his theory of permanent revolution, Trotsky miscalculated on two vital and connected points. He underestimated the ability both of capitalism to survive and of the USSR to keep afloat in a capitalist sea. This does not entirely invalidate his political theories, but it does make it difficult to argue that they represent a special insight into the nature of historical change. To be fair, Trotsky never claimed precise knowledge in regard to the timing of the phases of the dialectic. He always insisted that revolution would take an untidy and erratic course, 'two steps forward, one back'; this followed logically from the principle of uneven development. But it is fair for the observer to ask that there be accuracy of prediction at some point, otherwise the claim of Marxism to be scientific becomes void. The predictions which had sustained Trotsky since 1898 were not fulfilled. Whether they ever can be, as his apologists continue to assert, remains a matter of faith rather than of political science.

TROTSKY AND STALINISM
—

Trotsky fought against Stalinism not because it was brutal but because it was brutal for the wrong reasons. All the signs were that Trotsky would have used very similar means to those employed by Stalin to enforce his concept of revolution on the Bolshevik state. Trotsky's militarisation of labour, his savagery against the Kronstadt rebels in 1921, and the extreme methods he used to discipline the Red Army are vivid examples of this. Absolute authority was the necessary requirement of Bolshevik rule. Furthermore, long before Stalin imposed himself on the Party, Trotsky had abetted Lenin in the creation of the one party totalitarian state, with its secret police, show trials, and prison camps. The interpretation of Trotsky as the Communist with the human face, someone who would have led the Russian Revolution towards international democratic socialism, runs contrary to all the evidence. His defeat and exile by Stalin has given him a spurious, even romantic, image as the 'angel of enlightenment', the true revolutionary ousted by the tyrant, but his record as commissar in the period 1917-21 makes it difficult to sustain that view of him.

TROTSKY'S ISOLATION

Trotsky claimed to be an internationalist. He described himself as 'a citizen of the world', but this should not be taken to mean that he possessed a real understanding of other cultures and societies. Those who describe him as an urbane cosmopolitan have been misled by his apparent European sophistication. The fact was that, for most of his life, Trotsky was in a kind of limbo, cut off from Russia, living where he could rather than where he chose, and invariably disliked by the people among whom he dwelled. Despite living for long periods among other cultures and peoples, émigré revolutionaries seldom integrated. They invariably stayed in revolutionary coteries, insulated from genuine contact with the local population. It is this that gives the air of unreality to so much of what Trotsky said about worldwide revolution. His was not the type of open mind that broadens through experience. Everything he saw was filtered through his own revolutionary preconceptions. In that sense, he remained a fanatic throughout his life. This revolutionary detachment from political realities helps to explain why the Bolshevik Revolution made so little headway outside Russia. It was a product not of western-European radicalism but of Russian absolutism. It also explains the equanimity with which Trotsky and Lenin resisted the protests from European Marxists against the severity of Bolshevik rule in Russia. The divine right of the tsars to obedience from their people had simply been replaced by the dialectical absolutism of the CPSU.

TROTSKY'S LIMITATIONS

Three particularly damaging weaknesses may be identified in Trotsky: his natural air of intellectual superiority which his colleagues saw as arrogance; his suspect Menshevik past which made old-guard Bolsheviks distrust his genuine commitment to their cause; his Jewishness, which, in a society whose ingrained anti-semitism survived the revolution, made him the eternal outsider. Trotsky was very conscious of this last handicap. In 1917 when Lenin offered him the post of Deputy Chairman of *Sovnarkom*, Trotsky rejected it on the grounds that his appointment would be an embarrassment to Lenin and the government; he said it would 'give enemies grounds for claiming that the country was ruled by a Jew'. It has also to be said that Trotsky's own behaviour added to the characterisation of him as an outsider. Although he was obviously deeply involved in the activities of government and party, he often adopted the pose of the statesmen standing above the fray. This was more than simply an irritating manner; it went a long way to depriving him of a loyal following in the party. His undoubted gifts as propagandist, orator and theoretician were no substitute for a power base in the party.

THE CHARACTER OF THE RUSSIAN REVOLUTION
—

Historians are coming increasingly to emphasise the essentially Russian character of the Revolution. To revolutionary minds like Trotsky's it was not especially significant that the proletarian revolution had begun in Russia; after all *iskra* had to ignite somewhere. The whole point was that it was an international class movement, not a national one. That was the theory to which he held. Three quarters of a century later, historians observe that in practice it was only in Russia that such a revolution occurred. The Bolshevik revolution proved impossible to export. The so-called Marxist revolutions in eastern Europe after 1945 were imposed by Soviet force of arms and the Chinese Revolution in 1949 was very much a home-grown affair that owed little to Soviet concepts. One powerful argument is that despite all the dramatic changes that occurred on the surface there was in fact no Russian revolution. What happened was that a new breed of authoritarians simply replaced the traditional ones. Despite all the talk of a fundamental change of society, in reality the essential structure remained. 1917 was a palace revolution. After 1917, as before, a small, unrepresentative, privileged elite claimed the right of total control over the mass of the population, who, never having known or expected social or political liberties, resigned themselves to the situation as they always had. There had never been any politics in a meaningful sense in Russia. It was the lack of that tradition that enabled the Bolsheviks to impose themselves in the way that they did. Nicholas Berdiaev, who helped found an anti-Bolshevik organisation soon after the October Revolution, lamented 'All the past is repeating itself and acts only behind new masks'. Paul Milyukov, the Kadet leader and professional historian, made the same point:

> The international aspect of Bolshevism is due to its origin in a very advanced European theory [Marxism]. Its purely Russian aspect is chiefly concerned with its practice, which is deeply rooted in Russian reality and, far from breaking with the 'ancien regime', reasserts Russia's past in the present.

TROTSKY'S 'RUSSIANNESS'

Lenin and Trotsky were internationalists and it is customary among historians to emphasise this aspect. Yet we miss an essential point about them if we leave out their essential 'Russianness'. They were a product of a particular culture, which had made them what they were. Although they lived a large part of their pre-1917 careers abroad, and Trotsky enjoyed playing the role of cosmopolitan sophisticate, they never entirely lost their Russian roots. Their understanding and reading of politics was conditioned by their Russian preconceptions. One striking feature of this is their attitude towards the revolutionary process. Such was the nature of the Russia in which they grew up that to them change could be achieved only in violent cataclysm. It could not occur in any other way. This made Russian politics a volatile mixture of state brutality and revolutionary violence. Indeed, in a sense there were no politics in the Russian tradition. Concepts such as loyal opposition and the acceptance of compromise solutions were unknown. Two observers of the events of 1917 and after, one foreign, one Russian, emphasised how the Bolshevik Revolution could be understood only in a Russian context.

> The conditions in this highly-organised, industrially-centralised, politically compact and insular country, and medieval, semi-barbaric, loosely-organised and politically-infantile Russia is almost inconceivable to those who have not been there to see.
>
> (John S.Clarke in *The Communist*, 23 September 1920)

Bolshevism is a Russian word. But not only a word. Because in that guise, in that form and in those manifestations which have crystallised in Russia during nearly two years, Bolshevism is a uniquely Russian phenomenon, with deep ties to the Russian soul. And when they speak of German Bolshevism or of Hungarian Bolshevism, I smile. Is that really Bolshevism? Outwardly. Perhaps politically. Without the Russian soul. It is pseudo-Bolshevism.

(Boris Sokolov, in *Bolsheviks and Bolshevism*, 1919)

TROTSKY'S SENSE OF MORALITY
—

For Trotsky, the present was a means of reaching the classless society of the future.

We shall create one brotherly state on the land which nature gave us. This land we shall plough and cultivate on associative principles, turn into one blossoming garden, where our children, grandchildren and great-grandchildren will live as in paradise.

To be over-concerned with lessening the imperfections of today would delay the achieving of the perfection of tomorrow. Trotsky and his fellow revolutionaries were future-orientated. It is in this light that we can best understand Trotsky's particular sense of morality. Morals were not absolute; they took their value from their context. It is significant that when Trotsky used the word 'morality', he invariably prefixed it with the adjective 'bourgeois'. What he meant by this was that there were no fixed notions of right or wrong. As he bitingly put it:

Only contemptible eunuchs maintain that the slave-owner who, by deceit and violence, places a slave in chains is the equal before morality of the slave who, by deceit and violence, casts off his chains.

Trotsky's premise, taken directly from Marx, was that the ruling class of the day determined the received moral values of society. Therefore, with the bourgeoisie in control, the moral code which operated would simply be the formalising of the bourgeoisie's power. Right and wrong in this context were relative to the needs and aspirations of the bourgeoisie. One obvious example was that in societies dominated by the middle class, property and its defence became a main object of law enforcement. The 'haves' structured the law so that it preserved their position and privileges against the 'have nots'. By the same logic, when the proletariat were in power, as after 1917 they were, law would reflect the values and aspirations of the workers. Concepts of right and wrong were now to be judged in relation to whether an 'offence' forwarded or retarded the Revolution. Trotsky gave his full backing to the assertion by a Cheka police chief in 1918:

> Murder, lies and treachery are immoral and shameful if they are harmful to the cause of the proletarian revolution; these same lies, treachery and murder are moral and laudable if they serve this revolution.

TROTSKY AND STATE TERROR

It is against Trotsky's particular concept of morality that we can best understand his attitude towards the question of terror as state policy. According to his reading of the dialectic, after 1917 the Revolution had entered the phase of the dictatorship of the proletariat, that is to say the era in which the workers, having taken power, were engaged in a violent struggle against the forces of reaction. The nature of the struggle justified the workers and their representatives in using the most extreme methods to maintain their dominance and so prepare the way for the perfect society that was to follow. Trotsky acknowledged no duality between ends and means. The ends were contained in the sweep of history, which was the means. Were the workers or their government to show less than absolute commitment to persecution of their class enemies, they would be failing in their historical duty. Therefore, to allow thoughts of mercy or clemency to deter them would be a denial of their class function. Writing of his policies under war communism, Trotsky explained:

> Violent revolution was necessary because the undeferrable demands of history proved incapable of clearing a road through the apparatus of parliamentary democracy . . . Anyone who renounces terrorism in principle must also renounce the political rule of the working class . . . The extensive recourse, in the Civil War, to execution by shooting is to be explained by this one simple but decisive fact. Intimidation is a powerful instrument of both foreign

and domestic policy. The revolution kills individuals and thus intimidates thousands.

In this stark form Trotsky's justification and use of terror tactics seems very hard to accept, but we have always to remind ourselves that Trotsky like all true Marxist revolutionaries, was future-orientated. That is, he believed that the present time was simply a transitional phase of history that would usher in the final climactic, harmonious society. The equivalent in traditional morality would be the concept of life on earth as simply a preparation for eternity. Christians traditionally accepted the suffering in 'this vale of tears' because they were convinced that all would be remedied in God's perfect world that would follow the Final Judgement. This teleological interpretation of life is remarkably similar in Trotsky's thinking. The present had to be forced to serve the future. The terrorising of class enemies in the present could well be disturbing in emotional and social terms, but to allow this reaction to determine policy would be to give in to 'bourgeois morality'. When the revolution had been fully achieved violence would necessarily and naturally cease.

> The further we go, the easier it will get, the freer each citizen will feel himself to be, the more imperceptible will the coercive force of the proletarian state become.

Although Trotsky as a revolutionary often expressed such optimistic idealism, he seldom referred to the population of Russia in terms of genuine respect. This was not merely the contempt that intellectuals often feel towards those not as enlightened as themselves. His understanding of history led him to conclude that the Russians were an especially backward people who had never fully developed the notion of individual worth. This together with their lack of culture made the business of raising their proletarian consciousness a particularly difficult one.

> The Russian people never knew in the past either a great religious reformation like the Germans, or a great bourgeois revolution like the French. Out of these came bourgeois individuality, a very important step in the development of human personality in general ... The very necessity of acquainting tens of millions of grown-up people with the alphabet and the newspaper shows what

a long road must be travelled before you can speak of a new socialist culture.

It was such thoughts that underlay his destruction of the trade unions and his coercion of labour. As he wrote in the 1920s:

The road to socialism lies through the highest concentration of state power. Like a light bulb which, before extinguishing itself, flashes brightly, so the state prior to its disappearance takes the form of the dictatorship of the proletariat, i.e. of the most pitiless state, which coercively controls the life of the citizens in all its aspects

TROTSKY'S PURITANISM

Like so many committed revolutionaries, Trotsky was a puritan at heart. His puritanism expressed itself in a lack of a real sense of humour, which is another way of saying he lacked a sense of proportion. Life's pleasures, whether intellectual or sensual, were secondary to the cause of revolution. There were many times, of course, when he gave way to human emotion. Examples are his grief at the death of his children (two committed suicide and one was killed during Stalin's purges in the 1930s) and the depth of his affection for his second wife, the ever-loyal Natalya. But it was thoughts of revolution that consumed him. That is why he drove himself so hard throughout his life and was prepared to accept constant uncertainty, privation and exile. His selflessness in the cause of revolution is a fascinating example of the supremacy of intellect over feeling. Again one is drawn to religious comparisons. Trotsky has the intensity of those Christian saints who were prepared to sacrifice everything to their conviction. This did not prevent his indulging his vanity; contemporaries frequently remarked on the care he took over his appearance and dress-style. But in the end his view of life was dictated by his belief that human society was governed by scientific laws which it was his task, like that of all true revolutionaries, to understand and to apply.

Trotsky's tombstone in Mexico

Points to consider

1) How strong are the grounds for regarding Trotsky as a failure?
2) Identify Trotsky's major political weaknesses.
3) Was Trotsky's 'Russianness' an aid or a bar to his political career?
4) What is meant by describing Trotsky as being 'future orientated'?
5) By what arguments did Trotsky justify the use of state terror?
6) How accceptable is the notion of Trotsky as a 'puritan'?

BIBLIOGRAPHY

While no one book on Trotsky will ever command complete acceptance the following is a selective list of some of the more accessible studies of the man and his times.

Terry Brotherstone & Paul Dukes, (editors), *The Trotsky Reappraisal*, Edinburgh, 1992. A collection of 18 essays by leading international scholars, based on the papers they read to a conference, 'Trotsky After Fifty Years' at the University of Aberdeen in 1990. The book is a must for all those who want to be informed on the latest thinking on Trotsky. Many of the modern authorities listed in chapter 10 above contributed to the conference.

Pierre Broué, *Trotsky*, Paris 1988, The most modern study available. The writer's own political leanings are evident throughout, but his book has already been acknowledged as a major work.

Isaac Deutscher, *The Prophet Armed: Trotsky: 1879-1921*, London, 1954; *The Prophet Unarmed Trotsky: 1921-1929*, London, 1959; *The Prophet Outcast Trotsky: 1929-1940*, London, 1963. This three-volume study has been superseded at certain points by more recent works, but it remains the indispensable reference book.

Max Eastman, *Leon Trotsky: the Portrait of a Youth*, Greenburg, 1925. The first major attempt by a western writer to make Trotsky accessible to a non-Russian audience.

Irving Howe, *Trotsky*, Glasgow, 1978. A study of Trotsky's main ideas by a writer who regards him as 'a political Titan of the twentieth century'.

Michael Lynch, *Reaction and Revolutions: Russia 1881-1924*, London, 1992. *Stalin and Khrushchev: The USSR, 1924-64*, London, 1990. These books are useful introductions that help to put Trotsky in his historical setting. Both are in the Hodder & Stoughton *'Access to History'* series.

Nicholas Moseley, *The Assassination of Trotsky*, London, 1972. An interesting treatment which, as well as concentrating on the matter in the title, makes many worthwhile comments on Trotsky's career overall.

Alec Nove, *An Economic History of the USSR*, London, 1976. The most authoritative study of the economics of the Russian Revolution.

Robert Payne, *The Life and Death of Trotsky*, London, 1978. A clear, straightforward, account.

Richard Pipes, *The Russian Revolution 1899-1919*, London, 1990. *Russia Under the Bolshevik Regime 1919-1924*, London, 1994. That Pipes is no lover of Communism does not detract from these spendidly-readable analyses of the Revolution in which Trotsky was involved.

Leonard Schapiro, *The Communist Party of the Soviet Union*, London, 1970. Strongly critical of Trotsky, but balances the favourable view of him by such biographers as Deutscher and Segal.

Ronald Segal, *The Tragedy of Leon Trotsky*, London, 1979. This book has been heavily criticised for being too favourably disposed to Trotsky, but it does offer some stimulating ideas.

Victor Serge & Natalya Sedova Trotsky, *The Life and Death of Leon Trotsky*, London, 1975. An important account by two writers who were eyewitnesses to what they describe.

Leon Trotsky, *The History of the Russian Revolution*, London, 1985. Of the huge number of works written by Trotsky, this one (first published in 1933) probably provides the best compendium of his ideas. One of the values of this edition is that it is the translation by Max Eastman, who was also biographer of Trotsky and knew his subject personally.

Dimitri Volkogonov, *Trotsky*, Moscow, 1992. This book, which has not yet appeared in an English translation, provides an important source of revision in Trotsky's studies.

Bertram D.Wolfe, *Three Who Made a Revolution*, New York, 1948. An integrated biography of Trotsky, Lenin and Stalin, this is a very readable analysis of the great triumvirate of the Russian Revolution.

INDEX